Routledge
Taylor & Francis Group

LONDON AND NEW YORK

100590672

Eighth edition published 2012
by Routledge
2 Park Square, Milton Park, Abingdon, Oxon OX14 4RN

Simultaneously published in the USA and Canada
by Routledge
711 Third Avenue, New York, NY 10017

Routledge is an imprint of the Taylor & Francis Group, an informa business

© 2012 Routledge

First edition published by Cavendish Publishing Limited 1997
Seventh edition published by Routledge 2010

British Library Cataloguing in Publication Data
A catalogue record for this book is available from the British Library

ISBN: 978-0-415-68336-4 (pbk)
ISBN: 978-0-203-29999-9 (ebk)

Typeset in Rotis
by RefineCatch Limited, Bungay, Suffolk

MIX
Paper from
responsible sources
FSC® C004839
www.fsc.org

Printed and bound in Great Britain by
TJ International Ltd, Padstow, Cornwall

Contents

Table of Cases

Table of Statutes

TABLE OF STATUTES

How to use this book

Welcome to this new edition of Routledge Equity and Trusts Lawcards. In response to student feedback, we've added some new features to these new editions to give you all the support and preparation you need in order to face your law exams with confidence.

Inside this book you will find:

■ NEW tables of cases and statutes for ease of reference

■ Revision Checklist

We've summarised the key topics you will need to know for your law exams and broken them down into a handy revision checklist. Check them out at the beginning of each chapter, then after you have the chapter down, revisit the checklist and tick each topic off as you gain knowledge and confidence.

1

Sources of law

Primary legislation: Acts of Parliament	■
Secondary legislation	■
Case law	■
System of precedent	■
Common law	■
Equity	■
EU law	■
Human Rights Act 1998	■

■ Key Cases

We've identified the key cases that are most likely to come up in exams. To help you to ensure that you can cite cases with ease, we've included a brief account of the case and judgment for a quick aide-memoire.

HENDY LENNOX v GRAHAME PUTTICK [1984]

Basic facts

Diesel engines were supplied, subject to a *Romalpa* clause, then fitted to generators. Each engine had a serial number. When the buyer became insolvent the seller sought to recover one engine. The Receiver argued that the process of fitting the engine to the generator passed property to the buyer. The court disagreed and allowed the seller to recover the still identifiable engine despite the fact that some hours of work would be required to disconnect it.

Relevance

If the property remains identifiable and is not irredeemably changed by the manufacturing process a *Romalpa* clause may be viable.

■ Companion Website

At the end of each chapter you will be prompted to visit the Routledge Lawcards companion website where you can test your understanding online with specially prepared multiple-choice questions, as well as revise the key terms with our online glossary.

You should now be confident that you would be able to tick all of the boxes on the checklist at the beginning of this chapter. To check your knowledge of Sources of law why not visit the companion website and take the Multiple Choice Question test. Check your understanding of the terms and vocabulary used in this chapter with the flashcard glossary.

■ Exam Practice

Once you've acquired the basic knowledge, you'll want to put it to the test. The Routledge Questions and Answers provides examples of the kinds of questions that you will face in your exams, together with suggested answer plans and a fully-worked model answer. We've included one example free at the end of this book to help you put your technique and understanding into practice.

QUESTION 1

What are the main sources of law today?

Answer plan

This is, apparently, a very straightforward question, but the temptation is to ignore the European Community (EU) as a source of law and to over-emphasise custom as a source. The following structure does not make these mistakes:

■ in the contemporary situation, it would not be improper to start with the EU as a source of UK law;

■ then attention should be moved on to domestic sources of law: statute and common law;

■ the increased use of delegated legislation should be emphasised;

■ custom should be referred to, but its extremely limited operation must be emphasised.

ANSWER

European law

Since the UK joined the European Economic Community (EEC), now the EU, it has progressively but effectively passed the power to create laws which are operative in this country to the wider European institutions. The UK is now subject to Community law, not just as a direct consequence of the various treaties of accession passed by the UK Parliament, but increasingly, it is subject to the secondary legislation generated by the various institutions of the EU.

1

Equity and the nature and types of trust

A trust is a relationship which arises where one person (the trustee) is compelled in equity to hold assets for the benefit of another (the beneficiary) or for a purpose permitted by law.

THE ANATOMY OF A TRUST

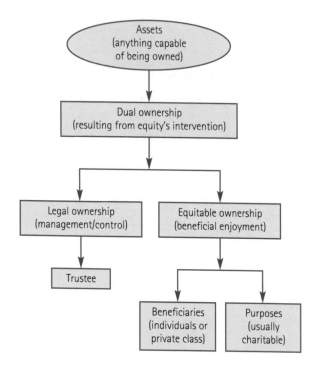

KEY ELEMENTS OF THE TRUST

ASSETS

Trusts are inextricably linked to assets. As Lord Browne-Wilkinson emphasised in *Westdeutsche Landesbank Girozentrale v Islington LBC* [1996], 'in order to establish a trust, there must be identifiable trust property'. Anything that is capable of being owned may constitute the assets.

EQUITABLE ORIGIN OF THE TRUST

The trust (or use as it was called) arose in the Middle Ages for a variety of reasons, for example as a way of avoiding feudal dues which were payable on death. By vesting legal ownership of property in two or more trustees, who could be replaced as they died, continuous ownership of the property could be secured and the feudal dues avoided.

From the outset, the common law courts refused to recognise the rights of the beneficiary who began to petition the King. In time, the King passed these petitions to his Chancellor, who could use his discretion and make such order as appeared to him to be fair or 'equitable'. The sittings of the Chancellor to hear the petitions became more regular and by the end of the 14th century had developed into the Court of Chancery. Gradually a doctrine of precedent began to develop for equity, just as it did for the common law.

There were thus two sets of courts, the common law courts administering the common law and the Court of Chancery administering equity. Both had their own particular procedure and remedies. During the 19th century, a number of reforms took place culminating in the Judicature Acts of 1873–1875 which replaced the common law courts and the Court of Chancery by one Supreme Court of Judicature in which each court had the power to administer both common law and equity according to the same rules of procedure. The orthodox view is that whilst the administration of the common law and equity were fused, the rules of common law and equity remain distinct. 'The two streams of jurisdiction, though they run in the same channel, run side by side and do not mingle their waters' per Lord Evershed.

THE MAXIMS OF EQUITY

The maxims of equity are basic principles developed by the Court of Chancery which are still applied by the courts as guidelines when exercising their equitable jurisdiction. The main maxims are as follows.

Delay defeats equities

The claimant who seeks an equitable remedy should not delay in taking action.

Equity is equality

Where two people have an equal claim to property, equity will order an equal division.

Equity acts *in personam*

Equity acts against the person and not *in rem*, ie equitable remedies are exercised against the person, for example an injunction may compel a person not to do something. A failure to comply is regarded as contempt of court punishable by imprisonment.

Equity looks to the intent rather than the form

Equity will give effect to the substance of the transaction rather than merely to its outward appearance.

Equity will not allow a statute to be used as an instrument of fraud

The court will not apply a statute which imposes formal requirements if strict compliance would be unjust by promoting the fraud of a litigant.

Equity will not allow a trust to fail for want of a trustee

If necessary, the court will appoint a trustee.

Equity will not assist a volunteer

Equity will not provide a remedy for a person who has not given consideration, for example the contractual remedy of specific performance would not be available to a volunteer. However, in relation to trusts, a beneficiary (even if he is a volunteer) will be afforded the protection of equity *provided* the trust is completely constituted (see later).

Equity will not perfect an imperfect gift

If a donor makes an imperfect gift (ie the donor does not comply with the requirements to transfer legal title to the property to the donee), equity will not perfect that gift.

He who comes to equity must come with clean hands

Equitable remedies are discretionary, and such a remedy will not be granted if the claimant has acted fraudulently or unconscionably.

He who seeks equity must do equity

A person seeking equitable relief must be prepared to act fairly towards the other party.

ENFORCEMENT OF THE TRUST

Where a trust is for individuals or a private class of persons, eg 'my employees', this entitles those persons to enforce the trustee's obligations, ie the beneficiary enforces a private trust.

Where the trust is for a purpose recognised by the law as charitable, and is exclusively charitable and for the public benefit, then it may be enforced by the Attorney General as a charitable trust.

The general rule is that a non-charitable purpose trust is void as there is no beneficiary to enforce the trust.

DUALITY OF OWNERSHIP

Under the common law, once trust property is vested in T, he is deemed to be the legal owner.

Equity does not dispute T's legal ownership but recognises B as the equitable owner of the trust property. In substance, this means that T is responsible for administering the trust property while B enjoys the benefits flowing from the property.

As Lord Browne-Wilkinson pointed out in the *Westdeutsche* case, the most notable consequence of such equitable ownership is that, 'once a trust is established, as from that date of its establishment, the beneficiary has, in equity, *a proprietary interest* in the trust property' [emphasis added]. The hallmarks of this interest are that:

- it is capable of being disposed of or acquired like any other interest in property;

- it may itself become the subject matter of a trust; for example, if T holds property on trust for B, B may declare himself a trustee of the interest for the benefit of Z (known as 'Sub-trust');

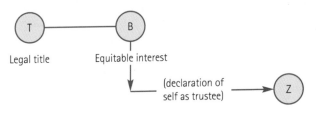

Legal title   Equitable interest

(declaration of self as trustee)

In the alternative, B may direct his trustee to hold his equitable interest on trust for Y (this may be a disposition under *Grey v IRC* [1960]).

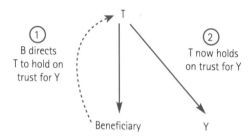

■ it is enforceable not only *in personam* against the trustee but *in rem* against the whole world except a *bona fide purchaser of the legal estate for value without notice*. For example, if T wrongfully transfers trust property to A, B has a personal claim against T for mismanaging the trust while his interest in the property continues to subsist against A.

CLASSIFICATION OF TRUSTS

PUBLIC TRUSTS AND PRIVATE TRUSTS

Public trusts		Private trusts	
Type of trust/gift	Enforceability	Type of trust/gift	Enforceability
(1) Trust for specified charitable purpose	Enforceable by AG	(1) Trust for persons	Enforceable by beneficiaries
(2) Donations to charitable bodies	Enforceable by AG	(2) Trust for non-charitable purposes	Not ordinarily enforceable but may be upheld if for upkeep of tombs/pets and trustee is willing
		(3) Gift to unincorporated non-charitable body	Depends on whether it is construed as being on trust for its purposes or a gift to its members

Public or charitable trusts

A charitable trust or a public trust is for a purpose which is recognised by the law as charitable, for example the relief of poverty. The trust must be for the public benefit and be exclusively charitable. Charitable trusts enjoy a number of legal advantages, for example they may be enforced by the Attorney General, and have many fiscal privileges.

Private trusts

A private trust is for the benefit of individuals or a specified group of persons, for example 'my grandchildren', and is enforceable by such beneficiaries.

Difficulties arise where a trust is created not for the benefit of ascertainable persons but for a stated purpose which is not charitable. These are called non-charitable purpose trusts. The general rule is that these trusts are void as there is no beneficiary to enforce them.

However, there are three exceptions when trusts for non-charitable purposes will be upheld – they are trusts for the erection and maintenance of monuments or graves; trusts for specific animals; trusts for the saying of private masses. These exceptions are said to be 'concessions to human weakness or sentiment' *Re Astor's Settlement Trusts* [1952] and are called trusts of imperfect obligation or unenforceable trusts. See *Re Dean* [1889] and *Re Hooper* [1932].

The problem of whether a trust/gift is for a purpose or for persons is particularly acute where property is given to an unincorporated association which does not have charitable purposes (see Chapter 9). Such a gift may be construed as giving rise to a trust for the association's purposes, in which case it is liable to fail as a non-charitable purpose trust. Alternatively, the gift may be construed as one to the members who collectively make up the association with the result that it will not fail for want of beneficiaries. As a rule, however, the individual members do not thereby acquire immediate distributive shares in the property given; rather it will be treated as an accretion to the association's assets to be applied for the benefit of the members. See *Leahy v AG for New South Wales* [1959]; *Neville Estates v Madden* [1962]; and *Re Recher's WT* [1972].

TYPES OF PRIVATE TRUST

Private trusts are divided into express trusts, resulting trusts and constructive trusts.

Express trusts

An express trust is created intentionally by the settlor (S) for the beneficiary (B).

An express trust arises as a result of a declaration of trust by the settlor. He may declare himself trustee, or he may declare the trust and transfer the trust property to another person to act as trustee. The first two examples below are *inter vivos* trusts (made between the living).

- S, the owner of Blackacre, declares himself trustee of the property for B;

- S, the owner of Blackacre, conveys it to Z on trust for B (these are *inter vivos* trusts and S is a settlor); or where

- T leaves Blackacre in his will to Z with directions to hold it on trust for B (this is a testamentary trust and T is the testator).

Fixed trusts, discretionary trusts and protective trusts are types of express trust (see below).

Resulting trusts

Traditionally there are two kinds of resulting trust

Automatic resulting trust

Such a trust is said to arise by operation of law, although it is argued that an automatic resulting trust gives effect to the settlor's presumed intention just as a presumed resulting trust does. Automatic resulting trusts arise in a number of circumstances, for example:

- where an express trust fails for some reason – *Re Diplock* [1941];

- where the settlor fails to dispose of the entire beneficial interest – *Vandervell v IRC* [1967];

- where an express trust comes to an end with surplus funds – *Re Abbott Fund Trusts* [1900].

In each of these cases, the trust fund will result back to the settlor. In the case of a testamentary trust or if the settlor is deceased, the fund will result back to the testator's estate and will be held for the residuary beneficiary under the testator's will, or if no such beneficiary, it will be held for the deceased's next of kin under the intestacy rules.

Presumed resulting trust
This type of resulting trust is clearly based on the presumed intention of the settlor. Such a trust would occur in the following situation.

■ Where property is purchased in the name of another. It is presumed that the property is held on presumed resulting trust for the purchaser. This presumption may be rebutted by evidence that the purchaser intended to make a gift.

Constructive trusts
In general terms, the constructive trust is the residual category of trust. Such trusts have, over the years, been imposed in a wide variety of situations in which the courts have found it necessary to compel a person to hold property for the benefit of another in the interests of justice and good conscience.

The following are examples of the types of situations in which the courts have been prepared to impose constructive trusts:

■ where a fiduciary misappropriates property entrusted to him or has made unauthorised profits;

■ where a third party knowingly receives trust property or is an accessory who dishonestly facilitates the trustee's breach of trust;

■ where a statute enacted to prevent fraud is fraudulently used by one person to enrich himself at another's expense;

■ where a person acquires legal title to property through killing another; or

■ in relation to claims to a beneficial interest in the family home.

Statutory trusts
Even where there is no express declaration of trust, there are several contexts in which trusts have been imposed by statute, for example:

9

- under s 33 of the Administration of Estates Act (AEA) 1925 (as amended by the Trusts of Land and Appointment of Trustees Act (TLATA) 1996) which provides that, where a person dies intestate, his personal representatives shall hold his real and personal property on trust with a power to sell it;

- under the Law of Property Act (LPA) 1925 (as amended by the TLATA 1996), statutory trusts of land are imposed:

  - where a legal estate is beneficially limited to or held on trust for any persons as joint tenants (s 36);

  - where land is expressed to be conveyed to two or more persons in undivided shares. Such persons (or the first four if there are more than four) hold as joint tenants under a statutory trust (s 34);

  - under s 27 of the Settled Land Act (SLA) 1925, which has been superseded by TLATA 1996, an attempt to transfer a legal estate to an infant is effective as a declaration of trust of land by the person purporting to make the transfer.

FIXED, DISCRETIONARY AND PROTECTIVE TRUSTS

These are types of express trust, ie they are created intentionally/expressly by the settlor/testator.

Fixed trusts

It is open to a settlor or testator in creating a trust to specify the precise beneficial interest to be taken by each intended beneficiary. The duty of the trustees is to distribute the trust property as directed, eg '£100,000 on trust for John and Jane equally'.

Discretionary trusts

Alternatively, S may leave it to T to determine the manner in which trust capital, income or both should be distributed. Where S does so, a discretionary trust arises, eg '£100,000 to be divided amongst such of my children as my trustees think most in need'.

The discretionary trust is considered an appropriate way of holding property for two reasons:

- it allows account to be taken of alterations in the circumstances of intended beneficiaries which may occur at a time when the settlor is no longer in a position to make required changes; and

- it provides a means of preventing the subject matter of the gift from being dissipated by a reckless beneficiary.

Protective trusts

The protective trust is known in certain jurisdictions as the *spendthrift trust*. It enables a balance to be struck between providing a beneficiary with a fixed share and encircling him with the safeguard of a discretionary trust.

The features of such a trust, as outlined in s 33 of the Trustee Act (TA) 1925, are:

- that it confers a fixed interest on the intended beneficiary either for life or for a specified period of a lesser duration;

- that this interest shall determine before running its full course on the happening of certain events such as bankruptcy or attempted alienation; and

- that, where the interest is determined, a discretionary trust will arise in favour of the intended beneficiary and his wife and children.

TRUSTS AND POWERS

A power is an authority given by a donor to a donee to deal with or dispose of the donor's property: see *Freme v Clement* [1881].

The most notable type of the power is the *power of appointment* under which the donee (or *appointor*) is authorised to appoint specified property to such persons (called objects or *appointees*) as the donee sees fit.

Powers	Trust
May be legal (eg, power of attorney) or equitable (eg, power of appointment)	Exclusively equitable
Discretionary in nature (may be carried out)	Imperative/obligatory (must be carried out)

With particular reference to powers of appointment:	By contrast, in the case of trusts:
◼ objects of power own nothing until power is exercised;	◼ beneficiaries become owners once trust is constituted;
◼ objects of power cannot compel donee to exercise power or transfer the property to them;	◼ beneficiaries of full age/absolutely entitled may demand trust property under rule in *Saunders v Vautier* [1841];
◼ if appointment is not made there will be gift over in default or resulting trust	◼ if trustee's duty to distribute is not carried out court will intervene to execute the trust

Trusts resemble powers in so far as both trustees and donees of powers are authorised to deal with or dispose of property belonging to the settlor or donor. There are, however, several significant differences between the two.

Over the years, however, the dividing line between trusts and powers has now become less clear cut as a result of the following developments:

◼ The modern trend towards conferring a wide range of powers and discretions on trustees by the trust instrument as well as by the various statutory provisions. These include ss 6–9 of TLATA 1996, and very wide powers in the Trustee Act 2000, such as s 3 – general power of investment and s 11 – power to employ agents.

◼ Powers which are conferred on trustees are called *fiduciary powers* and are distinguishable from *bare powers*, that is, those which are not held in a fiduciary capacity by the donee. In the case of a fiduciary power, the trustee is under a duty to consider from time to time whether to exercise it (see *Re May* [1982]); whereas the donee of a bare power is under no such duty.

◼ The judicial recognition of the resemblance between powers of appointment and discretionary trusts in *McPhail v Doulton* [1971], a case which, according to Pearce and Stevens, authors of *The Law of Trusts and Equitable Obligations*, 'marks the major break from the traditional dichotomy between trusts and powers'. This resemblance prompted Lord Wilberforce to remark on the narrowness and artificiality of the distinction between trusts and powers and ultimately persuaded him to adopt the same test for certainty of objects for powers and discretionary trusts.

❯ McPHAIL v DOULTON [1971] (a.k.a. Re Baden No 2)

Basic facts

A settlement created a discretionary trust to be applied for the benefit of 'officers or employees or ex-employees' of a particular company, and their families. It was argued that such a trust should fail for insufficient certainty of objects, it not being possible to make a complete list of beneficiaries.

Relevance

It departed from the test under *IRC v Broadway Cottages* [1955] and introduced the 'Any Given Individual' test to be applied to define objects under *'discretionary'* trusts. The Court held that having different tests for certainty in mere powers and discretionary trusts was '... arbitrary, illogical, and embarrassing ...'.

■ The superimposition of trusts on arrangements which would otherwise be regarded as powers in cases like *Burrough v Philcox* [1840]. This has resulted in the emergence of the *trust power* or *power in the nature of a trust.*

❯ BURROUGH v PHILCOX [1840]

Basic facts

The testator gave a life interest in property contained in a trust fund to his two children with remainders to their issue. The testator stated that if each of the children should die without leaving lawful issue then the survivor of the two children should have the power to dispose of the property by will among the testator's nephews and nieces, or their children 'as my surviving child shall think proper'. There was no gift over in default of appointment. The testator's two children did both die without leaving lawful issue.

Relevance

The court found that a trust and a power both existed. The property was initially subject to a power of appointment but that when the power was not exercised the intention was that the property should be distributed and that the class as a whole should benefit in any event. In other words, the court found a trust for equal division in default of the power being exercised.

The courts would carry out the general intention in favour of a class where there has been a failure to exercise a power of appointment and to select individuals from within that class.

■ The fundamental premise that trusts are imperative and powers discretionary has been eroded by:

- the willingness of the courts to give effect to *trusts of imperfect obligation*, which have no human beneficiaries who may compel performance;

- the acceptance in cases like *Mettoy Pensions Trustees v Evans* [1990] that, where a fiduciary power conferred on a trustee is not exercised by him, the court may intervene and execute the power.

SPHERES OF APPLICATION OF THE TRUST

According to Maitland, the trust is 'an institute of great elasticity and generality'. The truth of this assertion is borne out by the manner in which trusts have been employed in a wide variety of contexts. For instance:

■ the affairs of infants, persons of unsound mind, bankrupt persons, etc, are commonly placed in the hands of competent trustees;

■ the trust is frequently utilised as a device for preserving wealth within families (settlements, protective trusts, etc);

■ recourse is often had to secret trusts by persons who wish to provide for others without attracting publicity;

■ trusts have had a significant impact in the commercial sphere (for example, unit trusts and pension fund trusts);

■ where an unincorporated association acquires property it is usual for such property to be held by trustees on its behalf;

■ in the charitable domain, the trust serves as a vehicle for carrying out purposes beneficial to the community;

■ finally, trusts are central to numerous complex and ingenious *tax saving schemes* which have become commonplace in recent years.

You should now be confident that you would be able to tick all of the boxes on the checklist at the beginning of this chapter. To check your knowledge of Equity and the nature and types of trusts why not visit the companion website and take the Multiple Choice Question test. Check your understanding of the terms and vocabulary used in this chapter with the flashcard glossary.

2

Capacity and the three certainties

Does a minor have capacity to create a valid trust?

What are the three certainties?

Why are the three certainties needed?

What are precatory words?

What is the test of certainty of objects in a fixed trust?

What is the test of certainty of objects in a discretionary trust?

What is meant by conceptual uncertainty, evidential uncertainty and administrative unworkability?

What is the effect when a trust fails for uncertainty of subject matter?

What is the effect when a trust fails for uncertainty of objects?

There are four requirements to create a valid express trust:

- the settlor must have capacity to create a trust
- the three certainties must be satisfied
- the statutory formalities (if any) must be complied with
- the trust must be completely constituted.

Statutory formalities and complete constitution of a trust are dealt with in later chapters.

CAPACITY TO CREATE A TRUST

Basically, capacity to create an express trust depends on whether the settlor has the right to hold and dispose of a legal or equitable interest in property. Therefore any person over 18 who is not suffering from mental incapacity may create an express trust.

A person under 18 cannot hold a legal estate in land and therefore cannot create a trust of the same. With respect to express trusts of other property, these are voidable, ie they may be repudiated by the minor or within a reasonable time after he attains the age of 18.

THE THREE CERTAINTIES

Knight v Knight [1840]: In order for an express trust to be validly declared, three certainties must be present. These are certainty of intention, certainty of subject matter and certainty of objects.

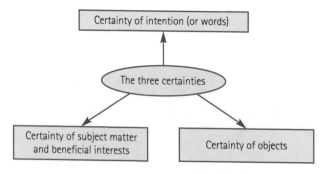

CERTAINTY OF INTENTION (OR WORDS)

Imperative words required: In declaring a trust, the settlor must use imperative words to indicate that he intends to impose an obligation on the trustee. The easiest way of manifesting this intention is to include the word 'trust' or 'trustee' in the declaration, for example, 'T on trust for B'. Even where the word 'trust' does not appear in the declaration, other imperative words (direct, require, instruct, etc) will usually suffice, for example, S transfers Blackacre to T and states that 'I direct him to hold it for B': see *Re Le Cren Clarke* [1995].

In the absence of words which are clearly imperative, complications may arise at two levels:

- In some instances, it may be difficult to determine whether a *trust* or a *power* was intended. For example, '£500,000 to X to be distributed among such of my nephews and nieces as X shall select':

  - if construed as a *trust* and X fails to select, the nephews and nieces will be entitled as a class;

▶ KNIGHT v KNIGHT [1840]

Relevance
Confirmed the three 'certainties' required for express creation of trust:

1 intention
2 subject matter
3 objects

The purpose of the test for certainty is to ensure that an express trust has not been created against the wishes of the owner of the property. The three certainties need to be satisfied so that the trust can be enforced and supervised by the court if necessary.

  - if construed as a *power of appointment* and X fails to select, the money will revert to the donor or his estate.

- In other instances, the difficulty may lie in determining whether a *trust* or an *outright gift* was intended. This is especially the case where a gift of property is accompanied by *precatory words* as opposed to imperative words. For example, X transfers property to Y declaring that he wishes (or hopes/

desires/suggests/believes) that Z will benefit from the property. Initially, the Chancellors took the view that gifts accompanied by precatory words imposed a trust on the donee: see, for example, *Harding v Glyn* [1739]; *Hart v Tribe* [1854]; and *Gully v Cregoe* [1857].

A new approach followed the Executors Act 1830 as signalled by *Lambe v Eames* [1871], which held that the use of precatory words in a gift did not mean that the donor intended the donee to hold the property on trust. This has been reinforced by other cases in which the courts have refused to enforce as trusts, gifts accompanied by precatory words. For example:

Case	Precatory words
Mussoorie Bank v Raynor [1882]	'Feeling confident'
Re Adams and Kensington Vestry [1884]	'In full confidence'
Re Diggles [1888]	'It is my desire'
Re Hamilton [1895]	'I wish them'
Re Williams [1897]	'In the fullest confidence'
Re Connolly [1910]	'I specifically desire'
Re Johnson [1945]	'I request that'

It is not, however, an absolute rule that a trust can never be created where precatory words are employed. Thus the words 'in full confidence' when considered in the context of the whole trust instrument were held to create a trust in *Comiskey v Bowring-Hanbury* [1905], whilst in *Re Adams and Kensington Vestry* [1884], the same precatory words 'in full confidence' were held not to create a trust when the will was construed as a whole. Therefore, the transferee took absolutely and not as trustee.

Inferring intention to declare trust
The courts have sometimes discovered an intention to create a trust from the settlor's conduct where no trust was specifically declared. For example:

Case	Circumstances from which trust was inferred
Paul v Constance [1977] *Rowe v Prance* [1999]	Repeated assertions by A to B that A regarded property to which trust relates as belonging to B as much as it does to A
Re Kayford [1975]	Trading company's segregation of money paid by customers ordering goods from the rest of the company's funds revealed an intention to create a trust
Dhingra v Dhingra [1999]	Bank account opened by father. Intention to create trust in son's favour inferred from the fact that bank statements recorded the account holder as being the father 'as trustee for' the son

UNCERTAINTY OF INTENTION

If, on construction of the words and conduct of the transferor, no trust is intended, the transferee who has acquired the property will be entitled to it beneficially.

CERTAINTY OF SUBJECT MATTER AND BENEFICIAL INTERESTS

There are two issues here. Firstly, the trust property must be certain and secondly there must be certainty as to the beneficial interest.

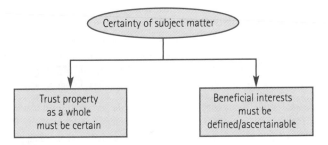

Certainty as to the trust property

A trust is liable to fail unless the property covered by it is properly identified. The test for certainty of trust property and beneficial interest is whether the subject matter is so precise that the court may attach a court order on the property or beneficial interest. Failure to satisfy the test may occur in the following contexts:

(a) *Where the property to be held on trust forms an undifferentiated part of a larger quantity:* This state of affairs is typified by *Re London Wine Co* [1986]. LWC, the owner of a large stock of wine, declared that it would hold parts of its stock on trust for various buyers without taking any steps to set apart the respective quantities to be held on trusts from the bulk of its stock. The trust was declared invalid partly on the principle that this failure to segregate the wine to be held on trust rendered the subject matter of the trust uncertain. This meant that on LWC's insolvency the buyers had no priority over its other creditors. See also *Re Goldcorp* [1994].

In *Hunter v Moss* [1994], however, the Court of Appeal declined to apply the principle in *Re London Wine Co* in circumstances where M, who owned 950 shares in a company, declared himself a trustee of 50 shares for H without specifying the shares. The trust was upheld as valid on the basis that the shares were intangible assets of identical value and so specific appropriation was not needed to make the subject matter of the trust certain. This was subsequently endorsed in *Re Harvard Securities Ltd* [1997]. However the distinction made between tangible and intangible property has been criticised, e.g. mass produced goods are often indistinguishable and a better distinction might be based on whether the trustee is solvent (as was the case in *Hunter v Moss*) or insolvent as in the case of *Re London Wine* and *Re Goldcorp.*

It is also noteworthy that, in the specific context of sale of goods transactions, the effect of *Re London Wine Co* has now largely been reversed by the Sale of Goods (Amendment) Act 1995. Under this Act, buyers of unsegregated consignments of goods forming part of a larger bulk are now collectively regarded as joint tenants of the legal title to the bulk and, as such, will have priority over the seller's other creditors in respect of such goods.

(b) *Where relative words are employed in defining the property:* Failure of a trust on this account is exemplified by *Palmer v Simmonds* [1854] which involved a gift by a testatrix of 'the bulk' of her residuary estate and *Re Kolb* [1962] which concerned a direction to hold 'blue chip securities' on trust. See also *Anthony v Donges* [1998] where the testator directed that his widow receive 'such minimal part of [the] estate as she might be entitled to under English law' – void for uncertainty. On the other hand, the expression 'residue' inserted in a will or trust instrument is regarded as sufficiently clear to satisfy the test for certainty of subject matter.

EXAM ISSUE: Students often get this wrong in examinations – 'residue' describes what is left after the estate has been finalised and is therefore TOTALLY CERTAIN!

Note, however, the more flexible approach in *Re Golay's WT* [1965] with regard to a trust to pay a reasonable income to a named beneficiary.

(c) *Where property is given to one person subject to a gift of an unspecified part of the property to some other person:* A gift of this nature was held to be uncertain in *Sprange v Barnard* [1789], where T left a sum of money for H directing that at H's death any part of this sum which he did not require was to go to X, Y and Z equally: see also *Curtis v Rippon* [1820].

▶ RE GOLAY [1965]

Basic facts

The testator made a will directing that a beneficiary was to '... enjoy one of my flats during her lifetime, and a reasonable income from my other properties'. Although it could be argued that this trust should fail owing to insufficient certainty of subject matter, in fact the Chancery Division upheld it.

Relevance

A 'reasonable income' held to be sufficiently exact to define *subject matter* of trust. The words 'reasonable income' provided the court with a yardstick to quantify the amount based on the personal circumstances of the beneficiary. (Compare – a trust/gift of a reasonable sum – which would undoubtedly fail for want of certainty as to the subject matter.)

The effect of failure to satisfy the test for certainty of trust property is that the transferee may retain the property beneficially.

A more accommodating approach, however, is evident in the context of *mutual wills* and *secret trusts*. These sometimes involve testamentary gifts of property to a person who is supposed to leave whatever part of it he has not utilised for himself in his lifetime to some other person. As seen from cases such as *Birmingham v Renfrew* [1937] and *Re Cleaver* [1981] (mutual wills) and

Ottaway v Norman [1972] (secret trust), the courts have endorsed such arrangements (which they characterise as 'floating trusts') despite the inherent uncertainty regarding their subject matter.

Certainty as to beneficial interests

A trust in favour of more than one beneficiary may fail because it is impossible to ascertain the interests to be taken by the beneficiaries. If the trust property is certain but the beneficial interest is uncertain, a resulting trust will arise in favour of the transfer. In *Boyce v Boyce* [1849], for instance, T left two houses to trustees who were to convey to his daughter M whichever one she chose and to hold the one not chosen by M on trust for his other daughter C. M died before choosing and the trust in C's favour failed because her interest was uncertain.

> ### ▶ BOYCE v BOYCE [1849]
>
> #### Basic facts
> The testator left four houses, one to be chosen by a certain beneficiary and the other three to go to another. In the event, the first beneficiary predeceased the testator, making it impossible to identify which three of the four houses should be settled. The court chose to uphold the principle that the precise beneficial interest should be determinable and the result was that neither beneficiary got anything.
>
> #### Relevance
> In this case, the uncertainty was not in the trust property – this was clearly the four houses – but in the beneficial interest to be assigned. Consequently, the effect of the uncertainty was a resulting trust in favour of the settlor's estate. This seems a harsh rule; the testator wished to dispose of four houses, and was not concerned which went to whom. His wishes could have been effected by allowing one house to go to his residual estate, chosen by his executor, leaving the other three to go to the named beneficiary.

A trust will not, however, fail on this account where a settlor or testator creates a discretionary trust under which the trustees are to determine the interests of the various beneficiaries; or where the court discovers a workable formula for distribution as in *Re Knapton* [1941], where lots were used to determine the entitlement of beneficiaries.

CERTAINTY OF OBJECTS

The objects of charitable trusts are the purposes for which they are created, while the objects of non-charitable (private) trusts are the intended beneficiaries. A non-charitable trust is effective only if these beneficiaries are ascertained or ascertainable.

Where there are no identifiable beneficiaries (for example, because the trust is essentially for a non-charitable purpose) the trust will fail as there will be no one to enforce it – see *Re Hummeltenberg* [1923] and *Re Astor's Settlement Trust* [1952].

As mentioned earlier, there are only three exceptions to this, when a non-charitable purpose trust will be upheld – see trusts of imperfect obligation.

Certainty of objects in the context of trusts for individuals

The requirement of certainty is easily fulfilled in the case of trusts for the benefit of named individuals, for example, '£10,000 to T on trust for Bill Bloggs'.

Where individual beneficiaries are not named but identified by description, the requirement is satisfied once an individual who fits the description can be identified, for example, '£1,000 to T on trust for the oldest person living on the Bleak Estate, Swansea'.

Trusts for a class of persons

Where a trust is not for specified individuals, but for a designated class, eg 'my employees', it can only be carried out if there is sufficient certainty to enable the trustees to tell who belongs to the class.

Where class gifts are concerned, uncertainty may be present:

- because the language used to describe the class is open to different interpretations (conceptual uncertainty); eg 'on trust for my friends'; or

- because the evidence needed to establish who belongs to the class is incomplete (evidential uncertainty), for example there is a practical difficulty in drawing up a list of beneficiaries, eg in a trust for all law students who graduated from Bartlett University in 2001, there would be evidential uncertainty if the records of past students of the university were destroyed in a fire.

The trust may also fail for administrative unworkability if the class is too wide thus containing too many potential beneficiaries for the trustees to handle (*R v District Auditors ex p West Yorkshire CC* [2001]).

In determining whether there is certainty of objects, the courts have distinguished between fixed trusts and discretionary trusts.

Fixed trusts

A fixed trust arises, for instance, where S transfers £100,000 to T on trust for S's brothers in equal shares. In this type of trust the trustee has no discretion regarding the amount to be given to each beneficiary, thus S's directions can only be carried out where the size of the class and identities of all the members are known to or capable of ascertainment by T.

The test for deciding whether the objects of such a trust are certain is to consider whether a *comprehensive list* can be made, which accurately includes the names of all those who are beneficially entitled, while excluding all those who fall outside the class: see *IRC v Broadway Cottages* [1955]; *Re Gulbenkian's ST* [1970]; and *McPhail v Doulton* [1971].

If a comprehensive list cannot be drawn up because the description of the class is conceptually uncertain, the trust will fail, for example, '£10,000 on trust for all my old friends in equal shares': see *Re Gulbenkian's ST* [1970] and *Brown v Gould* [1972]. But see also *Barlow's WT* [1979].

In *OT Computers Ltd v First National Tricity Finance Ltd and Others* [2003] the court decided that a trust intended for 'urgent suppliers' was void because it was not possible to identify each member of the specified class of objects.

Even where the class is described in terms which are conceptually certain, the trust will still fail if it is impossible to draw up such a list because there is evidential uncertainty.

Discretionary trusts

A settlor who declares a trust in favour of a class may opt not to fix the shares of individual members and give the trustee a discretion to determine these shares. Before 1970, the test for certainty of objects for discretionary trusts was the comprehensive list test applicable to fixed trusts: see *Re Ogden* [1933]; *IRC v Broadway Cottages* [1955]; and *Re Sayer* [1957].

The comprehensive list test was, however, discarded by the House of Lords in the landmark case of *McPhail v Doulton* [1971] which concerned a discretionary trust in favour of a certain Mr Baden's 'employees', 'ex-employees', their 'relatives' and 'dependants'. Their Lordships preferred the less stringent test formulated for powers in *Re Gestetner* [1953] and *Re Gulbenkian*. Under this test, the decisive criterion is whether the words employed in describing the discretionary class are such that it can be said with certainty that any individual *is or is not* a member of that class. The test is known variously as the is or is not test, the class test, the given postulant test.

The *Baden* saga did not end in the House of Lords since the case was remitted to the High Court, and thence to the Court of Appeal (under the name *Re Baden (No 2)*) to determine whether the reference to 'relatives' and 'dependants' rendered the trust uncertain. In determining this issue, all three Court of Appeal judges embraced the 'is–is not' test but each judge approached the test from a different perspective. Stamp LJ adopted a strict literal approach, arguing that for the test to be satisfied the trustee had to be able to say of *any* individual that he either is or is not within the class. He would not allow a class of 'don't knows'.

The test was construed less rigidly by Megaw LJ and Sachs LJ. The former signified that the test would be satisfied if, as regards a substantial number of objects, it could be said with certainty that they fell within the class even though, as regards a substantial number of others, it could not be proven whether they are within or outside the class. For his part, the latter maintained that whether or not a person fell within the class was a question of fact and, if a given claimant could not prove that he was within the class, then he could be taken to be outside it.

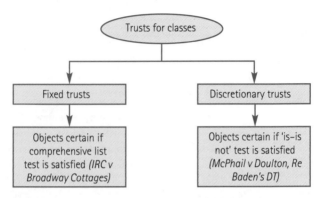

Curing uncertainty by reference to opinions of third parties

Where a trust would ordinarily fail, because the class of beneficiaries is defined in conceptually uncertain terms, will such a trust be rendered valid by the provision in the trust instrument of some mechanism for the trustee or a third party to determine the meaning to be ascribed to such terms?

Academic opinion is divided on this matter. Martin, author of Hanbury and Martin, *Modern Equity*, asserts that:

> . . . conceptual uncertainty may in some cases be cured by providing that the opinion of a third party is to settle the matter.

By contrast, others like Hayton, author of *The Law of Trusts* and Riddall, author of *The Law of Trusts*, maintain that conceptual uncertainty cannot be resolved by such provisions. According to Hayton:

> If the concept is my tall relations or my old friends or my good business associates and the trustees are given the power to resolve any doubt as to whether a person qualifies or not since the court cannot resolve this conceptual uncertainty it is difficult to see how the trustees can.

▶ Re TUCK'S SETTLEMENT TRUSTS [1978]

Basic facts
The testator left instructions that his baronetcy should only be inherited by an heir who married a woman of the Jewish faith.

According to his will, any doubts about the meaning of 'Jewish faith' were to be resolved by the Chief Rabbi. The question was whether this obligation was sufficiently certain that it could be enforced.

Relevance
Problems of conceptual uncertainty can be solved by referring the issue to a third party.

There is a similar divergence of judicial opinion. In *Re Tuck's Settlement Trust* [1978], Lord Denning saw no reason why a trust instrument should not provide that any dispute or doubt should be resolved by the trustees or others. See also *Re Leek* [1969]. This view does not appear to be shared by Jenkins J, who stated in *Re Coxen* [1948] that a gift will not be saved by making reference to the opinion of trustees where the testator (or settlor) has himself insufficiently defined the state of affairs on which the trustees are to form their opinion.

Trusts with a power of selection

As seen from *Burrough v Philcox* [1840] (in Chapter 1), a trust may sometimes be superimposed on a power of appointment, for example, if X empowers Y to distribute £100,000 among his nephews and nieces as he sees fit and directs that in default of distribution they are to take the £100,000 in equal shares. Where this happens, it appears that the test for powers/discretionary trusts will at the outset determine whether the class is sufficiently certain. If, in due course, Y defaults in making the selection, a fixed trust arises and the stricter test laid down in *IRC v Broadway Cottages* comes into play.

Gifts expressed to be subject to a condition precedent

Fixed trusts in favour of a class differ materially from trusts which confer a series of separate gifts on individuals who fulfil a condition or fall within a description, for example:

- if T is given £500,000 on trust to divide it equally among the settlor's old friends, this is a fixed trust in favour of a class which will fail for uncertainty of objects under the comprehensive list test. By contrast:

■ if T is given £500,000 and directed to pay £1,000 to each of the settlor's old friends, this gives rise to a series of individual gifts in favour of persons falling within this description. As seen from *Re Barlow's WT* [1979], the comprehensive list test does not apply to this type of trust.

The applicable test as laid down in *Re Allen* [1953] is that such a trust will not fail for uncertainty of objects once it is possible to say of at least one person that he or she satisfies the description of 'old friend'.

> ▶ Re BARLOW'S WILL TRUSTS [1979]

Basic facts

The testatrix made a will giving instructions to her executors that her collection of paintings was to be offered for sale at below-market price to 'friends of mine'. The question that arose was whether this clause was sufficiently certain that it could be enforced. The test, according to Browne-Wilkinson J, was whether it was possible to say, of 'one or more persons' that they qualified as 'friends of mine'. It was not necessary to define what a 'friend' is.

Relevance

This is a fairly broad test for certainty of objects arguably broader than any of those proposed by the Court of Appeal in *Re Baden (No 2)*.

The effect of uncertainty of objects is that a resulting trust arises in favour of the transfer.

The criteria for determining whether the objects of a trust are sufficiently certain may be summarised in the diagram opposite.

Criteria for determining whether the objects of a trust are sufficiently certain

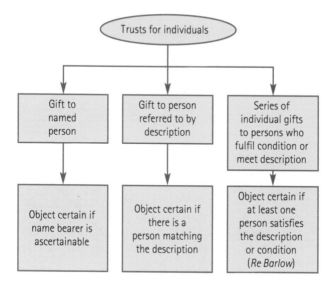

Fixed trusts	Discretionary trusts
List of beneficiaries required	Apply 'the is or is not test', ie is it possible to say with certainty of any given applicant that he is or is not a member of the class of beneficiaries
Trust will fail if beneficiaries conceptually uncertain	
Trust will fail if there is evidential uncertainty	Trust will fail for conceptual uncertainty but not evidential uncertainty
Trust will fail if administratively unworkable	Trust will fail if administratively unworkable

You should now be confident that you would be able to tick all of the boxes on the checklist at the beginning of this chapter. To check your knowledge of Capacity and the three certainties why not visit the companion website and take the Multiple Choice Question test. Check your understanding of the terms and vocabulary used in this chapter with the flashcard glossary.

Statutory formalities

3

What formalities are required under s 53(1)(b) Law of
Property Act 1925 when a trust of land is declared?

What formalities are required under s 53(1)(c) LPA when there
is a disposition of a subsisting equitable interest?

Give examples of dispositions of subsisting equitable interests

What is the effect of non-compliance with s 53(1)(b) LPA?

What is the effect of non-compliance with s 53(1)(c) LPA?

What types of trust are exempt under s 53(2) LPA?

Secret trusts

What are the differences between a fully secret trust and a
half secret trust?

When do these trusts arise?

What is the theoretical basis for upholding secret trusts?

What are the rules of communication for a fully secret trust?

How do these rules compare with those for a half secret trust?

What is the rule in *Re Stead*?

Can a secret trustee take as secret beneficiary?

Can a secret beneficiary witness the will?

What happens when a fully secret trust fails?

What happens when a half secret trust fails?

STATUTORY FORMALITIES FOR CREATION OF EXPRESS TRUSTS

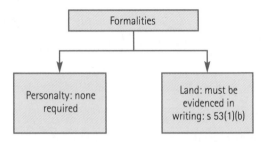

A person who wishes to create an express trust must ensure that he observes any formal requirements imposed by statute. There are different requirements for *inter vivos* (come into being while settlor is still alive) and testamentary trusts (set up by the testator's will and come into being on his death).

INTER VIVOS TRUSTS

Trusts of personalty
Where the owner of personal property sets out to declare a trust of such property, he is not obliged to comply with any formal requirements. The effect of this, as pointed out by Dillon J in *Hunter v Moss*, is that 'it is well known that a trust of personalty can be created orally'.

But, note that different considerations apply where the person creating a trust of personalty is the equitable owner of the property while legal ownership resides elsewhere (see disposition of a subsisting equitable interest below).

Trusts of land
Where the subject matter of a trust is land, writing has been an important requirement since the enactment of the Statute of Frauds 1677. It has long been the case that a purchaser of land which is held on trust must pay the purchase price to at least two trustees. The use of writing, where a trust relates to land, reduces the likelihood of inadvertent non-compliance by a purchaser with the 'two trustee' rule ('overreaching').

The requirement of writing is now embodied in s 53(1)(b) of the Law of Property Act (LPA) 1925 which provides that a declaration of trust respecting land or an interest in land must be manifested and proved by some writing signed by some person able to declare the trust. See, for example, *Bristol and West Building Society v Pritchard* [1994].

The following points should be noted with regard to s 53(1)(b):

- The actual declaration need not be in writing provided it is evidenced in writing. The evidence may be supplied in several documents. A document acknowledging a prior oral declaration will suffice, as seen from *Forster v Hale* [1798]; *Childers v Childers* [1857]; and *McBlain v Cross* [1871].

- The document must show that a trust was intended but need not contain all its terms: see *Re Tyler's Fund Trust* [1967].

- The document must be signed by the person able to declare the trust (that is, the owner of the land or interest which is the subject matter of the trust). An agent's signature will not suffice: see *Re Northcliffe* [1925].

- The requirement of writing was introduced to prevent fraud and the courts will not allow it to be used as a cloak for fraud, as seen from cases like *Rochefoucauld v Bousted* [1897]; *Bannister v Bannister* [1948]; and *Hodgson v Marks* [1971].

- Non-compliance with s 53(1)(b) LPA renders the trust unenforceable.

Statutory formalities on the disposition of subsisting equitable interests (ie disposing of an existing trust interest)

The owner of an equitable interest in property may confer the benefit of the interest on another person by:

1 assigning the interest directly to a third party;
2 directing the trustees to hold the property in trust for a third party;
3 contracting for valuable consideration to assign the interest to another; or
4 declaring himself to be a trustee for another.

These principles were laid down by Romer LJ in *Timpson's Executors v Yerbury* [1936].

Section 53(1)(c) of the LPA 1925 provides that a *disposition* of an equitable interest or trust *subsisting* at the time of the disposition must be in writing, signed by the person disposing of the same or by his agent thereunto lawfully authorised in writing.

The following points should be noted with regard to s 53(1)(c):

■ Under s 53(1)(c), the disposition must be in writing. Evidence in writing of a prior oral disposition will not suffice.

■ The document disposing of the equitable interest need not be signed by the owner. It may be signed by his agent.

■ Section 53(1)(c) applies not only to equitable interests in land (see *Ivin v Blake* [1995]) but also to equitable interests in personalty: see *Grey v IRC* [1960] and *Vandervell v IRC* [1967].

■ Failure to comply with s 53(1)(c) LPA will render the disposition void.

■ **EXAM ISSUE:** The use of the word *subsisting* is significant. It means that where the owner of a legal estate or interest in property declares a trust this will not be governed by s 53(1)(c) since this involves creating a new equitable interest rather than disposing of a subsisting equitable interest.

Dispositions which fall within the ambit of s 53(1)(c)

The owner of an equitable interest may enter into a variety of transactions and arrangements involving his interest. The courts have been called upon from time to time to determine which of these transactions and arrangements qualify as dispositions within the meaning of s 53(1)(c). The position in this regard may be summarised as follows.

Type of transaction/arrangement	Is it a disposition which must be in writing under s 53(1)(c)?
Assignment of subsisting equitable interest to trustee	Yes
Direction to trustee with legal title to hold subsisting equitable interest on trust for third party	Yes: *Grey v IRC*
Direction to trustee with legal title to transfer property to third party	Amounts to a transfer of legal and equitable title so need not comply with s 53(1)(c): see *Vandervell v IRC*
Declaration of new trust by resulting trustee with consent of equitable owner	Upheld in *Re Vandervell (No 2)* despite non-compliance with s 53(1)(c)

Specifically enforceable contract to assign subsisting equitable interest	Not clearly settled in *Oughtred v IRC* whether such contract is a disposition which must be in writing. However, minority view of Lord Radcliffe that such a contract passes an equitable interest under a constructive trust even if oral has been endorsed by CA in *Neville v Wilson*
Declaration by owner of subsisting equitable interest of himself as trustee	Passive trust regarded as disposition under s 53(1)(c) but not active trust
Disclaimer of beneficial interest	Not a disposition under s 53(1)(c) according to *Re Paradise Motor Co*; *Allied Dunbar v Fowler*
Nomination of death benefits under pension scheme or life insurance policy	Not a disposition under s 53(1)(c) according to *Re Danish Bacon Co*; *Gold v Hill*

1. Assignment of the interest directly to a third party

Settlor

|

Trustee

|

Beneficiary 1   … assigns his subsisting equitable interest to Beneficiary 2

Where beneficiary 1 assigns his interest to beneficiary 2, this is clearly the disposition of a subsisting equitable interest. It is therefore necessary for beneficiary 1 to comply with s 53(1)(c) LPA. Failure to comply would mean that the transaction is void and beneficiary 1 would still own the equitable interest.

2. Direction to trustees to hold the property in trust for a third party

Where the equitable owner of property (which is held on trust for him by a trustee as his nominee) directs his trustee to hold the property on trust for a third party, then this is a disposition of a subsisting equitable interest and must comply with s 53(1)(c) LPA.

This is illustrated by *Grey v IRC* [1960].

> ▶ **GREY v IRC [1960]**
>
> Basic facts
>
> The settlor wished to transfer shares to trustees for his six grand-children. To avoid the use of a document (if made in writing it would attract stamp duty) he first transferred the legal title to the trustees of his grandchildren's trust, to hold on bare trust for himself. Because the settlor retained the same benefit of the shares (originally as legal owner, now as exclusive beneficiary under the bare trust) no *beneficial interest* was transferred, and no stamp duty payable.
>
> He then instructed the trustees to transfer the benefit of the trust to his grandchildrens' trusts, in equal shares. He argued that this was not a 'disposition' of an equitable interest, and hence did not require a document.
>
> The trustees in due course wrote to the Revenue, indicating that they held the shares on trust for the grandchildren.
>
> The IRC argued that the oral instruction to hold the shares for different beneficiaries amounted to a disposition, and was therefore void because it should have been in writing. They also argued that the later letter from the trustees amounted to the disposition of an equitable interest, and should therefore attract stamp duty. The House of Lords agreed on both points, and ruled that the trusts were valid and stamp duty was payable.
>
> Relevance
>
> The direction to a trustee to hold trust property for another is a 'disposition' under s 53(1)(c) LPA 1925.

3. Transfer of both the legal and equitable interests to a third party

Trustee (holding as nominee) ⟶

Beneficiary ⟶   ⟶ Third Party

Where the beneficiary under a bare trust directs the trustee to transfer both the legal and equitable interests to a third party, this does not constitute a disposition of a subsisting equitable interest and may be effected orally, ie s 53(1)(c) LPA does not apply. The case which illustrates this is *Vandervell v IRC* [1967].

▶ VANDERVELL v IRC [1967]

Basic facts

The settlor wished to sponsor a professorship in the Royal College of Surgeons (RCS).

He was *equitable* owner of a substantial number of shares but the *legal* interest in Vandervell's shares was held by a bank as nominee.

In order to endow the Chair, he arranged with the bank *orally* (to avoid stamp duty) to transfer *both legal and equitable interests* in these shares to the Royal College of Surgeons (RCS), giving a trustee company (Vandervell Trustees Ltd., which he controlled) an option to re-purchase them for £5,000 (well under the value of the shares). This enabled the RCS to receive dividends but because of the option to re-purchase, Mr Vandervell did not irrevocably relinquish control of his shares.

At this stage, therefore, the legal and equitable interest in the shares had been transferred to the RCS. This raises a formalities point.

The IRC argued that:

1 Vandervell had made a valid transfer of the stock to the RCS, despite disposing of his equitable interest without writing, and
2 he had a beneficial interest in the option to purchase, which was extremely valuable. Consequently Vandervell had substantially *increased* his tax liability.

The House of Lords agreed on both counts. As to (1), it was held that an instruction to transfer the legal title out of a trust completely did not amount to a disposition of an equitable interest, *as in this case both legal and equitable title were transferred at the same time.*

So s 53(1)(c) of the LPA 1925 did not apply and writing was not required, and he was not liable to tax on this point.

However, on (2) because of the exercise of the option to purchase the company stock, the trust company had to apply those benefits for somebody else. Unfortunately, the beneficiaries of that trust (of the benefits of the option) were never declared, the trust failed for lack of certainty of objects, Vandervell had not divested himself absolutely of the shares which he controlled and the beneficial interest came back to him as an Automatic Resulting Trust.

Relevance

Conveyance of legal estate by trustee on direction of beneficiary is NOT a disposition under s 53(1)(c) LPA 1925.

The settlor must ensure that he fully divests himself of all benefit under any trust.

4. Termination of resulting trust and declaration of new trust with consent of the beneficial owner

This transaction is illustrated by the sequel to the above case – *Vandervell Trusts (No 2)* [1974].

▶ VANDERVELL TRUSTS (NO 2) [1974]

Basic facts

In 1961, Mr Vandervell directed the trustee company to exercise the option to repurchase the shares which had been transferred to the Royal College of Surgeons. The trustee company used £5,000 from a trust fund which already existed to benefit Mr Vandervell's children. Thereafter, they paid the dividends arising from the shares into the children's trust fund. They also informed the Inland Revenue that they were holding the shares on trust for the children.

Some years later in 1965, to resolve any doubts in the matter, Mr Vandervell executed a deed of release expressly declaring that the shares were held on trust for the children. Mr Vandervell died in 1967. He made no provision for his children in his will as he believed that he had provided for them under the trust.

The Inland Revenue claimed that Mr Vandervell had not disposed of his beneficial interest in the shares in writing as required by s 53(1)(c) LPA until he executed the deed of release and was liable for tax until that time.

The Court of Appeal held that neither the termination of the resulting trust of the option nor the creation of the new trust of shares for the benefit of the children, nor the two together, amounted to a disposition of a subsisting equitable interest within the meaning of s 53(1)(c) LPA 1925.

Relevance

s 53(1)(c) LPA 1925 does not apply where a resulting trust terminates and a new trust of personal property is declared by a trustee (in the above case by the trustee company) with the consent of the beneficial owner. Note that if the property involved is land, then the declaration of the new trust of land would have to comply with s 53(1)(b) LPA.

5. Oral contract to assign a subsisting equitable interest

Where O owns an equitable interest which he orally agrees to assign to B for valuable consideration, judicial opinions are divided on whether s 53(1)(c) is applicable. Such an arrangement arose in *Oughtred v IRC* [1960], where it was argued that a specifically enforceable oral contract by the owner of an equitable interest in shares to transfer these shares conferred an equitable interest on the transferee without any need to comply with s 53(1)(c). While this argument did not prevail in the House of Lords in this case, the reasoning behind it has since been accepted in other contexts in *Re Holt's Settlement* [1969]; *DHN Food Distributors v Tower Hamlets LBC* [1976]; *Chinn v Collins* [1981]; and *Neville v Wilson* [1996].

6. Equitable owner declares himself to be a trustee for another

It is not conclusively settled but it seems that if the equitable owner (beneficiary 1) declares that henceforth he is holding his interest on trust (a sub-trust) for another (beneficiary 2), then provided beneficiary 1 has active duties as trustee of the sub-trust, this is not a disposition of an equitable interest and there is no need for compliance with s 53(1)(c) LPA – *Grainge v Wilberforce* [1889].

It is argued that if beneficiary 1 has no active duties as trustee and effectively disposes of his interest to beneficiary 2, then beneficiary 1 is regarded as having 'dropped out' of the picture. He is in effect disposing of his beneficial interest and must comply with s 53(1)(c) LPA 1925. However, following *Nelson v Greening & Sykes (Builders) Ltd* [2008] which did not in fact involve s 53(1)(c), doubt has been cast on whether such a beneficiary does in fact drop out of the picture because, as a matter of law, he does not cease to be a trustee.

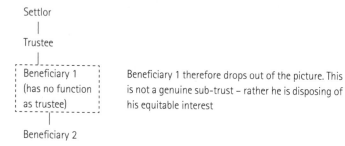

Settlor
|
Trustee
|
Beneficiary 1
(has no function
as trustee)
|
Beneficiary 2

Beneficiary 1 therefore drops out of the picture. This is not a genuine sub-trust – rather he is disposing of his equitable interest

7. Disclaimer of beneficial interest

It emerges from cases such as *Re Paradise Motor Co* [1968] and *Allied Dunbar v Fowler* [1994] that where a person who would otherwise be entitled to an equitable interest disclaims his interest this will not be caught by s 53(1)(c) since disclaimer operates by way of avoidance and not by way of disposition.

8. Nomination of death benefits

Where a member of an occupational pension scheme or the holder of a life insurance policy nominates a person who will receive benefits in the event of his death, this does not operate as a disposition under s 53(1)(c), as seen from cases such as *Re Danish Bacon Co* [1971] and *Gold v Hill* [1998].

Exceptions to the rules of formality

s 53(2) Law of Property Act 1925 provides that the formalities laid down in s 53 shall not affect the creation or operation of resulting, implied or constructive trusts, ie the formalities considered above regarding s 53(1)(b) and s 53(1)(c) are dispensed with if the circumstances point to the existence of a resulting or constructive trust. This was the case, for instance, in *Yaxley v Gotts* [2000] which involved an oral 'gentlemen's agreement' between Y and G, whereby Y was to undertake extensive renovation work on all the flats in a building owned by G and would, in return, be given two ground floor flats. G sought to resist Y's claim to these flats, contending that their agreement was not in writing as dictated by s 2 of the Law of Property (Miscellaneous Provisions) Act 1989. The Court of Appeal, however, upheld Y's claim on the ground that the agreement gave rise to a constructive trust.

In line with the foregoing, s 53(2) of the LPA 1925 states that the formal requirements prescribed in s 53(1)(b) and (c) do not apply to the creation of resulting, implied or constructive trusts. The effect of this exclusion is evident in cases like *Bannister v Bannister* [1948] and *Neville v Wilson* [1996].

In *Bannister*, X agreed to sell her cottage to Y for less than its value and in return Y orally declared that he would allow X to live in the cottage rent free. It was held that Y held the cottage on constructive trust for X even though there was no evidence in writing as required by s 53(1)(b).

In *Neville*, the shareholders of a family company agreed to dissolve it and distribute the shares among themselves in the proportion of their shareholding. The Court of Appeal held that the agreement constituted each shareholder an implied trustee of the shares for the other shareholders and was not required to be in writing as required by s 53(1)(c).

TESTAMENTARY TRUSTS

STATUTORY FORMALITIES FOR TESTAMENTARY GIFTS/TRUSTS

A person who wishes to create a trust that will take effect on his death is required by s 9 of the Wills Act 1837 to execute a formal will. Essentially, the will must be in writing, signed by the testator in the presence of two witnesses who also sign the will.

SECRET TRUSTS AND THE FORMALITIES REQUIREMENT

As stated above, the general rule is that a testamentary gift or trust must be stated in a valid will. There is an exception to this rule, namely secret trusts. A will is a public document and secret trusts usually arise where the testator wishes to make provision on his death for a person or purpose which he wishes to keep secret.

A secret trust typically comes into being where a testator (T) leaves property in his will to a devisee (D) or a legatee (L) and instructs D or L to hold the property on trust for the benefit of a beneficiary (B) who is not mentioned in the will. While the common law does not recognise B's interest if it is not embodied in the will, equity is able to give effect to T's intention by enforcing the trust against D or L. There are two types of secret trusts, namely:

Fully secret trust (FST)	Half secret trust (HST)
Where the existence of a trust is not manifest in the will, for example, T's will gives '£5,000 to L' but before executing it T tells L to hold the sum on trust for B	Where trust is declared in the will without disclosing objects, for example, T leaves Blackacre 'to D on trust for persons communicated to D' before executing the will

Note: Where T states in his will that L is to apply the property in a manner communicated elsewhere, but uses precatory language in the will, there will not be an HST. A FST may, however, arise if the communication outside the will is expressed in imperative terms: see *Re Spencer's Will* [1887].

Conditions for the enforcement of the FST

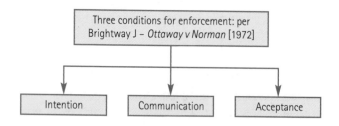

(a) *Intention*: T must manifest an intention to impose a binding obligation on L to hold the property left to him on trust for B. If T's words suggest that it is open to L to decide whether or not to apply the property for B's benefit, there will be no FST: see *McCormick v Grogan* [1869]; *Re Snowden* [1979]; and *Kasperbauer v Griffith* [1997].

(b) *Communication*: T must in his lifetime communicate his intention to L either before or after the will is executed. If not, L can claim the property beneficially: see *Wallgrave v Tebbs* [1865].

Where T conveys his intention to create the trust to L but does not in his lifetime communicate its terms and a letter containing the terms emerges after T's death, *Re Boyes* [1884] decided that the FST will fail. But note that, if T gives L a sealed letter containing the terms not to be opened by L until T's death, this is *constructive communication* and the FST will not fail.

(c) *Acceptance*: L will be bound by the FST only if he has undertaken to carry it out. Acceptance is usually express, but the courts may also imply acceptance on the basis of tacit acquiescence, where T's intention has been communicated to L who remains silent: see *Moss v Cooper* [1861] and *Ottaway v Norman* [1972].

Where there is no acceptance because T's intention was not communicated, L can take the property beneficially: see *Wallgrave v Tebbs* [1865].

The position is less certain where communication is made to L who refuses the trust but T nevertheless leaves the property to him. It is not entirely clear whether, in such an event, L is bound to hold the property on a resulting trust for T's estate or becomes beneficially entitled to the property.

Once L accepts the terms communicated by T, any additions to the objects or subject matter proposed by T will be enforceable only if duly communicated and accepted: see *Re Colin Cooper* [1939].

(d) *Certainty of subject matter*: The property subject to the secret trust must be certain – *Ottaway v Norman* [1972].

ACCEPTANCE WHERE THERE ARE TWO OR MORE LEGATEES/DEVISEES
Where T in his will leaves property to L1 and L2 intending that they should hold it as co-trustees for B, problems will arise if the trust is communicated to and accepted by L1 but not L2. The applicable principles are to be found in *Re Stead* [1900].

According to *Re Stead*, the position depends on whether the property has been left to them as joint tenants or tenants in common.

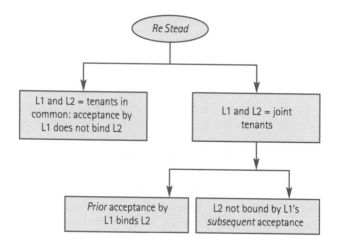

Where the property is left to L1 and L2 as tenants in common (for example, 'To L1 and L2 in equal shares'), each of them is deemed to have a separate and distinct interest in the property. Accordingly, where L1 alone accepts the trust, L2 will not be bound by it.

Where L1 and L2 are joint tenants (for example, 'To L1 and L2 jointly' or 'To L1 and L2') and L1 alone accepts the trust before the will is executed this will bind L2. By contrast, if L1 accepts after execution, L2 will not be bound by this.

CONDITIONS FOR THE ENFORCEMENT OF THE HST

The HST was judicially recognised only comparatively recently in the leading case of *Blackwell v Blackwell* [1929]. A HST, like a FST, is enforceable only where intention, communication and acceptance are present.

(a) *Intention*: A HST can only arise where T's intention to impose a trust is declared with sufficient certainty in the will itself.

(b) *Communication*: A HST which is not effectively communicated to the intended trustee will fail. The issue of communication was addressed in *Re Keen* [1937], which laid down two fundamental principles, as follows:

(1) the manner of communicating the objects/purposes to the intended trustee which is specified in the will must be consistent with the manner in which such communication actually occurs; and

(2) in any event, communication of the objects/purposes of the trust must occur before or at the time the will is executed.

See also *Blackwell v Blackwell* and *Re Bateman's WT* [1970]. In the judicial sphere, Carnwarth J expressed reservations about the prior communication rule in *Gold v Hill* [1998], where he referred approvingly to the suggestion in Snell's *Principles of Equity* that, 'in principle, there seems to be no real reason why the communication of the trust at any time before the testator's death should not suffice for the half secret as well as the fully secret trust'.

(c) *Acceptance*: A HST is liable to fail if the intended trustee does not accept that he will hold the property on trust for the beneficiary. This does not, however, entitle the trustee to take the property beneficially since he is obliged to hold it on a resulting trust for the testator's estate.

EXAM ISSUE: *Re Stead* decided that acceptance by one of two joint tenants before the execution of the will makes a FST enforceable against the other. The courts are yet to pronounce on the position where the same situation occurs in the context of an HST. It may, however, be inferred from *Re Stead* that the HST will be enforceable against the trustee who did not accept since: (1) it is usual for trustees under a HST to hold as joint tenants; and (2) communication of the trust must be before the will is executed.

CAN THE SECRET TRUSTEE TAKE AS A SECRET BENEFICIARY?
The problem with the half secret trustee claiming that he was also named by the testator as a secret beneficiary is that evidence of such a claim contradicts the terms of the will – *Re Rees' WT* [1950]. The decision in this case may turn on the fact that the half secret trustee was the testator's solicitor and had prepared the will. *Re Tyler* [1967] suggests that evidence is admissible regarding all the terms of the secret trust, including evidence that the half secret trustee is to benefit, although such evidence will not be lightly admitted.

Compare a fully secret trust – *Irvine v Sullivan* [1869].

POSITION WHERE INTENDED TRUSTEE PREDECEASES TESTATOR OR DISCLAIMS THE GIFT

In the case of a HST, the death of the trustee in the testator's lifetime or his renunciation of the trust will not invalidate the trust even if he was the sole trustee named in the will. The equitable maxim that a trust will not fail for want of trustees applies with full rigour in such cases.

The position is less clear cut where a FST is involved. On the one hand, Cozens-Hardy indicated in *Re Maddock* [1902] that such a trust will fail if the legatee/devisee dies in the testator's lifetime or disclaims the gift. This may be contrasted with *Re Blackwell* [1925], where Lord Buckmaster took the view that, where the evidence pointed to a FST, such a disclaimer or renunciation would not cause the trust to fail (although he did not comment on the effect of the intended trustee dying before the testator).

EXAM ISSUE: THE BASIS FOR THE ENFORCEMENT OF SECRET TRUSTS

(a) *The fraud theory*: The traditional justification adopted by the courts for enforcing secret trusts is the prevention of fraud. See the judgment of Lord Westbury in *McCormick v Grogan* [1868] and Lord Sumner in *Blackwell v Blackwell* [1929].

One variant of the fraud theory is that, unless the trust is upheld, the legatee/devisee will take the property beneficially, thereby unjustly enriching himself. This is not entirely convincing on two grounds:

■ it is arguable that unjust enrichment can equally be prevented by means of a resulting trust for the testator's estate; and

■ preventing unjust enrichment is immaterial in the case of a half secret trust which by its nature does not allow a trustee to take beneficially.

Another variant of this theory is that the fraud stems not from possible unjust enrichment but from the fact that, unless the trust is upheld, the testator's wishes will be thwarted and the beneficiaries will forgo their entitlements: see, for example, *Riordan v Banon* [1876]; *Re Fleetwood* [1880]; and *Blackwell v Blackwell* [1929].

(b) *The 'dehors' theory*: An alternative explanation for enforcing secret trusts is now widely accepted in judicial and academic circles. This is that they are not in fact created in the will but arise *dehors* (that is, outside and independent of) the will.

This presupposes that the trust is declared *inter vivos* when the relevant communication and acceptance occur and thus it need not comply with the formalities in s 9 of the Wills Act 1837. The function of the will is to *vest* the property in the trustee, thereby enabling the beneficiary to enforce the trust against him. Two cases vividly illustrate the operation of the *dehors* theory:

- **EXAM ISSUE:** *Re Young* [1951]: which held that s 15 of the Wills Act 1837, which prevents a witness to a will from taking a benefit under it, did not deprive a beneficiary under a secret trust of his entitlement on account of having witnessed the will; and

- **EXAM ISSUE:** *Re Gardner (No 2)* [1923]: which held that the interest of a beneficiary under a secret trust did not lapse where the beneficiary had died before the testatrix, as it would have done if the trust had arisen under the will rather than outside it.

The decision in *Re Gardner* has been criticised on a number of grounds, eg the decision would suggest that once the testator has declared the secret trust, he cannot revoke his will, or dispose of the property subject to the secret trust. Yet the secret trust is not completely constituted until the property is vested in the secret trustee, ie on the death of the testator.

ARE SECRET TRUSTS EXPRESS TRUSTS OR CONSTRUCTIVE TRUSTS?

This issue has generated considerable debate:

- Writers like Pettitt and Oakley favour the view that they should be treated as express trusts.

- By contrast, judges like Brightman J in *Ottaway v Norman* [1972], Nourse J in *Re Cleaver* [1981] and Moritt J in *Re Dale* [1993] refer to them as constructive trusts and this is echoed by Hodge.

- Other commentators like Hayton and Marshall suggest that HSTs are undoubtedly express trusts, whereas FSTs which have been traditionally associated with the fraud theory can properly be regarded as constructive trusts.

EXAM ISSUE: The express-constructive trust debate is especially relevant where a secret trust relates to land because under s 53(1)(b) communication of the trust must be evidenced in writing if it is express but not if it is constructive.

The position has not yet been judicially resolved but note:

■ *Re Baillie* [1886]: HST unenforceable in the absence of writing.

■ *Ottaway v Norman* [1972]: FST based on oral declaration upheld without regard to the possibility that s 53(1)(b) might render it unenforceable. See also *Brown v Porau* [1995].

The enforcement of secret trusts is ultimately a matter of policy. Secret trusts are not consistent with the certainty which the Wills Act 1837 was intended to provide.

You should now be confident that you would be able to tick all of the boxes on the checklist at the beginning of this chapter. To check your knowledge of Statutory formalities why not visit the companion website and take the Multiple Choice Question test. Check your understanding of the terms and vocabulary used in this chapter with the flashcard glossary.

Constitution of a trust

4

How is a trust constituted?

Contrast *Milroy v Lord* with *Re Rose*

What is meant by the maxim 'Equity will not assist a volunteer'?

Can a beneficiary enforce an incompletely constituted trust?

What remedies exist for a beneficiary of an incompletely constituted trust (a) in equity (b) at Common Law and (c) under Statute?

What are the three exceptions to the maxim that Equity will not perfect an imperfect gift?

What is meant by the rule in *Strong v Bird*?

What are the requirements for a *donatio mortis causa*?

What are the key elements of proprietary estoppel?

THE CONSTITUTION OF TRUSTS

Once an intention to make an outright gift or create a trust is declared, it must be determined whether the gift or trust is completely constituted. It is completely constituted when the property is transferred to, and becomes vested in, the donee or trustee. Where there has been a declaration but no vesting, the gift or trust is incompletely constituted.

THE SIGNIFICANCE OF VESTING

■ Where vesting has occurred, the donor/settlor can no longer change his mind and reclaim the property: see *Re Bowden* [1936].

■ In addition, the donee/beneficiary obtains an enforceable interest in the property even if he gave no consideration. See, for example, *Jeffreys v Jeffreys* [1841] and *Paul v Paul* [1882].

■ Where there has been no vesting, unless a donee/beneficiary has furnished consideration, he has no basis in equity for enforcing the trust against the donor/trustee.

EXAM ISSUE: This is reflected in the general rule that *equity will not assist a volunteer to perfect an imperfect gift:* see *Milroy v Lord* [1862]. An illustration of the type of situation in which the rule may come into effect was given by Lord Goff in *White v Jones* [1995], namely, where an *inter vivos* gift fails because the instrument transferring the property is defective. If the donor has, in the meantime, changed his mind, the donee cannot compel him to execute a new instrument since equity will not perfect an imperfect gift.

CONSTITUTION WHERE SETTLOR DECLARES HIMSELF A TRUSTEE

Where a person declares himself a trustee of his own property for the benefit of another, the trust will be completely constituted when the declaration is made since the property will already be vested in the settlor. This is so even if the intended beneficiary is unaware of the declaration: see *Middleton v Pollock* [1876] and *Standing v Bowring* [1885].

The following points should be noted with regard to self-constitution:

- Where the subject matter of the trust is land, s 53(1)(b) of the LPA 1925 requires the declaration to be in writing or evidenced in writing.

- Writing is also required where the person declaring himself a trustee owns only an equitable interest in the property concerned if this qualifies as a disposition under s 53(1)(c).

- Where a trust is declared with some other person as the trustee but vesting has not occurred, the beneficiary cannot seek to enforce the trust by claiming that the settlor declared himself a trustee: see *Milroy v Lord* [1862]. By the same token, if a donor sets out to make an outright gift but does not vest the property in the donee, the gift will not be enforced on the basis that the donor declared himself a trustee: see *Jones v Lock* [1865]; *Richards v Delbridge* [1874]; and *Hemmens v Wilson Browne* [1993] but compare the following Court of Appeal case – *Shah v Shah* [2010].

▶ SHAH v SHAH [2010]

Basic facts

Mr Dinesh Shah signed a letter that disposed of shares in favour of his brother and which was delivered with a signed stock transfer form but without the share certificate. He subsequently alleged that the letter was not effective for the purpose of vesting legal title to the shares in his brother as the letter was a gift and not a declaration of trust and the gift was not completely constituted and therefore of no effect as equity will not perfect an imperfect gift.

The court stated that legal title to a share in a limited company may only be transferred to another person by registration of the transfer of the share in the prescribed form. Therefore it may take time to complete a gift by registration of the shares in the donee's name but one of the ways to make an immediate gift was for the donor to declare a trust.

The Court of Appeal held that in interpreting a document, such as the letter, the court should not have regard to the subjective intention of its maker but to the intentions of the maker as manifested by the words he used in the context of all the relevant facts. In the present case, Mr Dinesh Shah used the words 'I am holding' not 'I am giving or I am assigning' and the concept that he held the shares for his brother could only be given effect in law by the imposition of a trust. Further, in his letter he described the document as a declaration with was more consistent with it being a declaration of trust than a gift.

CONSTITUTION WHERE SETTLOR IS NOT THE TRUSTEE

Where a settlor opts to create a trust with someone else as trustee (or an outright gift is made) it is completely constituted when the property is transferred to the trustee (or donee). The law lays down different modes of transfer for various types of property.

DIFFERENT MODES OF TRANSFER FOR VARIOUS TYPES OF PROPERTY

Property	Mode of transfer
Legal estates in land (that is, freeholds/leases for three or more years):	By deed (s 52 of the LPA 1925)
Chattels:	By delivery (note, in particular, Re Cole [1964]) or by deed (see Jaffa v Taylor Galleries [1990])
Company shares:	By memorandum of transfer in the form contemplated by s 1 of the Stock Transfer Act 1963)/ss 770–772 of the Companies Act 2006, coupled with registration of shares. See: Milroy v Lord [1862]; Trustee of Pehrsson's Property v Van Greyerz [1999]. See also Re Rose [1952]. But, note that the introduction of electronic share transfers in 1996 has meant that share transfer forms (but not registration) are now dispensed with in the case of certain plcs
Choses in action:	By assignment in accordance with the procedure in s 136 of the LPA 1925
Equitable interests:	By disposition in writing (s 53(1)(c) of the LPA 1925)

CONSTITUTION WHERE SETTLOR AND OTHERS ARE DECLARED TRUSTEES

Where a settlor declares himself one of several trustees and manifests an immediate and irrevocable intention to create a trust of specific property, a perfect trust is created. This is the position even though the settlor fails to transfer the property to the third party trustees. The office of trusteeship is joint and several and the retention by the settlor of the property as trustee is equivalent to all the trustees acquiring the property. This principle was decided by the Privy Council in *Choithram v Pagarani* [2001].

▶ T CHOITHRAM INTERNATIONAL SA v PAGARANI [2001]

Basic facts

Mr Pagarani, who was terminally ill, decided to establish a charitable foundation to receive his deposit balances and company shares, and appointed himself and nine others as trustees.

He subsequently signed a deed establishing the foundation and orally declared that he was giving all his wealth to the foundation. However, he died before any transfer of shares had taken place.

On Mr Pagarani's death intestate, his family claimed that the transfers were ineffective and were therefore part of his estate to which they as next-of-kin were entitled.

The Court of Appeal of the British Virgin Islands held that there was no trust as there had been neither an effective declaration of himself as trustee by Mr Pagarani nor an effective transfer of the shares to the trustees.

On appeal to the Privy Council, it was held that the foundation (an unincorporated association) was not a legal entity and therefore any property given to the foundation could only be held for it by the trustees of the foundation. Lord Browne-Wilkinson stated that there was no difference between the situation where a settlor declares himself as the sole trustee and where he declares himself as one of a number of trustees as in the present case. It did not matter that the shares had not been formally transferred to all the trustees because they were vested in one trustee, namely

Mr Pagarani, which the effect of constituting the trust. In the words of Lord Browne-Wilkinson 'it would be unconscionable and contrary to the principles of equity to allow such a donor to resile from his gift'.

EXCEPTIONAL SITUATIONS WHERE VESTING IS DEEMED TO HAVE OCCURRED IN EQUITY

(a) *Where the donor/settlor has made every effort:* At common law, property does not vest unless the formalities governing transfer are satisfied in the minutest detail. Equity, however, recognises that vesting takes place once a donor/settlor has done everything in his power to divest himself of the property even if the law requires some further task (such as registration) to be performed by a third party: see *Re Rose* [1952] and *Mascall v Mascall* [1985] but contrast with *Re Fry* [1946] and *Zeital v Kaye* [2001]. See also *Pennington v Waine* [2002], where the Court of Appeal seems to have relaxed the requirements further by holding the gift of shares assigned in equity by the execution of a share transfer form without delivery to the donee or company. The basis for the judgment was that it would be unconscionable to permit the donor to recall the gift.

▶ Re ROSE [1952]

Basic facts

Mr Rose wished to give 10,000 shares to his wife. On 30th March 1943, a completed share transfer form and the relevant share certificates were forwarded to the company. However, registration of the transfer by the company did not take place under 30th June 1943.

When Mr Rose died, the question for the court was whether the gift of the shares was subject to estate duty. This applied to gifts made within five years of a donor's death, i.e. in this case to gifts made for five years from 10th April 1943.

The Court of Appeal held that the effective date of the transfer of the shares was 30th March 1943 – the date when Mr Rose had done everything in his power to transfer the shares to his wife. The transfer was valid in equity from that date although not valid in law until registration by the company had taken place.

The rule in *Re Rose* is sometimes called the every effort rule.

▶ ZEITAL v KAYE [2010]

Basic facts

The case concerned the imperfect gift of a share in a company by Raymond Zeital to his companion, Stefka. Unlike the donor in *Re Rose*, Raymond was only the beneficial owner of the share while the legal owner was a Mrs Kumar.

The only way he could have transferred his beneficial interest to Stefka was by creating a sub-trust of his beneficial interest, or by assigning his subsisting equitable interest to her in writing in accordance with s53(1)(c) Law of Property Act 1925.

Further, the whereabouts of the share certificate were unknown and whilst Raymond could have asked the legal owner, Mrs Kumar, to obtain a duplicate he had not done so. Therefore Raymond had not done all in his power to transfer the share to Stefka (compare *Re Rose*) and therefore the gift failed.

▶ PENNINGTON v WAINE [2002]

Basic facts

Ada Crampton owned 1,500 of 2,000 shares in a private company. She wanted to give her nephew 400 of these shares and also wished him to act as a director of the company, which he could only do if he became a shareholder.

She instructed the company auditor, Mr Pennington, to prepare a share transfer form, which she duly completed and returned to Mr Pennington for him to secure registration.

Harold agreed to become a director and signed the necessary consent forms and was told by Mr Pennington that he need take no further action. However, a member of Mr Pennington's staff had placed the share transfer form on the company file and no action was in fact taken to secure registration prior to Ada's death a month later.

It was clear that unlike Mr Rose (see above), Ada had not done everything in her power to transfer the shares because the share transfer form had not been passed by her or her agent (Mr Pennington) to the transferee, Harold, nor had it been passed to the company for registration.

Nevertheless, the Court of Appeal held that given Harold's agreement to become a director which required the transfer of shares to him, it would be unconscionable for Ada to have recalled the gift and therefore the transfer was effective in equity. In the words of Arden LJ: 'There can be no comprehensive list of factors which makes it unconscionable for the donor to change his or her mind: it must depend on the court's evaluation of all the relevant considerations.'

The decision in *Pennington v Waine* has been widely criticised as undermining the strict rules applying to imperfect gifts on the broad basis of what a court might consider to be unconscionable.

(b) *Where vesting occurs by other means:*

(1) Where a donor expresses an intention to make an immediate gift of property but dies not having transferred it to the donee, the gift will ordinarily founder on the principle that equity will not assist the donee to perfect the gift. The donee may, however, be in a position to claim the property if he is able to rely on the rule in *Strong v Bird* [1874] (see below). As explained in *Collier v Calvert* [1994], the effect of this rule is that:

> ... where the donor maintains an intention to make a gift but does not perfect it and dies having appointed the donee

personal representative of the estate so that legal title vests on the death of the donor in the donee, [equity's] assistance is no longer required to order the transfer of the legal title to the donee. In view of the continuing wishes of the donor in such circumstances, no one has a better equity than the donee. So equity refuses to intervene against the donee.

(2) Where S declares his intention to transfer property to T to hold on trust for B and the property becomes vested in T in a different capacity, it emerges from *Re Ralli's WT* [1964] that the rule in *Strong v Bird* [1874] applies by analogy so that T will be able to enforce the trust on B's behalf. (Contrast, however, with *Re Brook* [1939].)

CIRCUMSTANCES IN WHICH A GIFT IS ENFORCEABLE WITHOUT VESTING

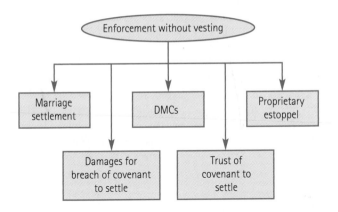

When the trust property has not been vested in the trustee, the trust is sometimes described as incompletely constituted. The beneficiary cannot enforce it as a trust but, depending on the circumstances, he may have contractual rights – see marriage settlements, specialty contracts, Contracts (Rights of Third Parties) Act 1999 below. Alternatively, the beneficiary may be able to claim that there is a completely constituted trust of a covenant, or in the case of an imperfect gift, he may be able to rely on one of the exceptions to the maxim that Equity will not perfect an imperfect gift. These are considered in turn below.

Marriage settlements

Where S promises to settle property on T pursuant to a marriage settlement (rare these days) and the marriage takes place but vesting does not occur, equity allows T to enforce the trust on behalf of the spouses and their issue: see *Pullan v Koe* [1913]. The reason for this is that equity regards the spouses and issue as having given notional consideration by virtue of the marriage. They are said to be 'within the marriage consideration' and may seek specific performance of S's promise.

The children of either spouse from an earlier marriage are volunteers but may have an enforceable interest in the property, provided the interest of such children are closely linked with those of the issue of the marriage: see *AG v Jacobs-Smith* [1895].

Where the marriage settlement provides that the property is to pass to the next-of-kin or some other third party if the spouses die without issue, such a party does not come within the marriage consideration. The trustees cannot therefore enforce the trust on his behalf where vesting has not occurred: see *Re D'Angibau* [1880]; *Re Plumptre's Marriage Settlement* [1910]; and *Re Pryce* [1917]. This is in line with the maxim Equity will not assist a volunteer.

Enforcement of covenants to settle under the common law

A covenant is a promise to transfer property which is under seal. Equity will not enforce the covenant by decreeing specific performance if it is not supported by consideration: see *Jeffreys v Jeffreys* [1841]; *Re D'Angibau* [1880]; and *Re Ellenborough* [1903]. The reason is that Equity does not recognise a specialty contract (ie a promise contained in a deed traditionally under seal).

By contrast, the common law will enforce the covenant against the covenantor without requiring consideration from the covenantee. For example, if A and B execute a voluntary deed under which A covenants to transfer property belonging to him to B, but fails to transfer it, B may recover damages against him: see *Cannon v Hartley* [1949].

Enforcement under the Contracts (Rights of Third Parties) Act 1999

Suppose the settlor covenanted with trustees to settle property on an identified beneficiary but failed to settle the property as promised. The covenant with the trustees is a specialty contract (ie a promise in a deed unsupported by consideration). Section 1 of the Contracts (Rights of Third Parties) Act provides that an identifiable third party to a contract (such as the beneficiary in the above example) may enforce any term of that contract provided the term in question purported to confer a benefit on him. A third party is identifiable if he is named or if he is a member of an identified class, eg 'my grandchildren'.

However, the third party remains a volunteer and thus is not entitled to an equitable remedy. He is therefore only entitled to claim damages.

The Act applies to specialty contracts made on or after 11 May 2000.

Example: S covenants with trustees to settle his ABC shares on his nephews. S fails to settle the shares. S's nephews are an identifiable class and were intended to benefit from the covenant. Therefore as third parties to the contract, they may rely on the Act and seek to enforce the contract by an action for damages.

Enforcement in equity where there is a trust of the covenant
Where there is a voluntary covenant by S to settle property on T on trust for B, T may not be willing to enforce the covenant. B may, however, be able to do so if he shows that S intended the right to sue on the covenant to be held on trust for B. In this event, the right to sue is treated as a *chose in action* and the trust of this *chose in action* becomes completely constituted when the covenant is made, even if the property which S covenanted to settle on trust has not yet been transferred to T (*Fletcher v Fletcher* [1844]).

It was, however, subsequently held in *Re Cook* that even if a trust of a covenant is enforceable where it relates to specific property or a sum of money, this will not be the case where it concerns future property.

Exceptions to the maxim that Equity will not perfect an imperfect gift
When a donor makes an imperfect gift, ie fails to vest legal title to the property in the donee, the donee cannot rely on Equity to perfect the gift unless the transaction falls within one of the three exceptions. They are the rule in *Strong v Bird*, *donatio mortis causa* (a death bed gift) and proprietary estoppel.

(a) The rule in Strong v Bird
The Rule in *Strong v Bird* enables an imperfect gift to be perfected if the donee of the gift is appointed as executor of the donor's will and if the donor had a continuing intention until death to make the gift. The rule has developed over the years and originated with the release of a debt.

▶ STRONG v BIRD [1874]

Basic facts

A stepson borrowed £1,100 from his stepmother. The stepmother lived in her stepson's house and paid quarterly board. It was agreed that the stepson would repay the debt of £1,100 by deducting £100 from the quarterly board paid by his stepmother but, after two reduced payments, the stepmother stated that she did not want the loan repaid and thereafter until her death, she paid the full board.

At common law, the release of the debt by the stepmother should have been under seal but this formality was never complied with, i.e. at law, it was an imperfect release of a debt. However, the stepmother appointed her stepson as her executor which had the effect on her death of vesting legal title to the debt in him, thereby releasing the debt.

The rule in *Strong v Bird* was extended to imperfect gifts in *Re Stewart* [1908] and in *Re James* [1935] was further extended to a donee who was appointed administratrix on the death of an intestate donor. The decision in *Re James* has been criticised because whereas an executor is appointed by a conscious and deliberate act of the donor, an administrator applies to court for letters of administration to administer the intestate's estate.

The donor must have an immediate intention to make an inter vivos gift (compare *Re Freeland* [1952] where the intention was to make gift in the future), and that intention must have continued up to the date of the donor's death.

In *Re Gonin* [1979], a mother expressed her intention to give her house to her daughter, who had given up her job to look after her parents. The daughter was illegitimate and the mother mistakenly believed that she was unable to leave the house to her daughter in her will so instead she drew a cheque for £33,000 in her daughter's favour. The mother died intestate and her daughter applied for letters of administration. The cheque for £33,000 in favour of the daughter was discovered after the mother's bank account had been frozen and the cheque was accordingly worthless. The daughter claimed that her mother had intended her to have the house and that on her appointment as administratrix of her mother's estate, the imperfect gift was perfected. However, it was held that the mother did not have a continuing intention in respect of the house as her intention had changed when she drew the cheque in favour of her daughter.

There are dicta in *Re Wale* [1956] that the rule in *Strong v Bird* could be applied to perfect an incompletely constituted trust if the would-be trustee is appointed as executor of the settlor's estate. However, caution is required here because the rule in *Strong v Bird* applies only to specific identifiable property where there is an intention to make an immediate gift, so for example it would not apply to a covenant to settle unidentified property at some future date.

(b) A donatio mortis causa (DMC)

A DMC is a gift made in the donor's lifetime but expressed to be conditional on and intended to take effect on his death. It is neither an *inter vivos* gift in the strict sense, nor is it a testamentary gift which must comply with the formalities laid down in the Wills Act 1837: see *Re Beaumont* [1902].

EXAM ISSUE: According to Russell CJ in *Cain v Moon* [1896], three conditions must exist for a DMC to be valid:

1 the gift must be in contemplation of the donor's death;
2 the donor must intend the property to revert to him if he does not die; and
3 the subject matter of the DMC (or the means of gaining control of it) must be delivered to the donee.

Regarding the first condition identified above, it is irrelevant if the donor dies from a cause other than that which he was contemplating. Thus in *Wilkes v Allington* [1931], the fact that the donor had contemplated dying of cancer but in fact died of pneumonia did not affect the validity of the death bed gift.

Regarding the second condition, if the donor was contemplating death, e.g. from a serious illness, but recovered, the death bed gift would be automatically revoked. The donor may, of course, expressly revoke the gift during his lifetime but he cannot revoke the gift by will as the death bed gift would already be complete, i.e. on the donor's death. Note therefore that a death bed gift prevails over the will.

Regarding the third condition, if the subject matter is a chattel and it has been delivered to the donee or he has been given the means of gaining access to it (such as the key to the place where it is kept), the donor's death perfects the gift: see, for example, *Woodard v Woodard* [1991]. In *Re Lillingston* [1952] the donee was given a key to a trunk which contained jewellery and a further key to a Harrods safe deposit box. The Harrods safe deposit box contained a key to yet another safe deposit box. It was held that there was a valid death bed gift of the jewellery and the contents of the two safe deposit boxes.

In *Woodard v Woodard* [1995] a terminally ill father in hospital gave his son the keys to his car so that the son could drive his mother to visit the hospital. The father subsequently told the son on several occasions that he should keep the keys as he would not be driving the car again. It was held that the father's conversation had changed the son's position from bailee of the car to that of donee of a death bed gift. It was irrelevant to the issue of dominion that there might be a second set of keys at the donor's home as the father was not in a position to use a possible second set.

If the subject matter is such that delivery would not suffice to constitute an *inter vivos* transfer, title to the property will not vest automatically in the donee/trustee on the donor's death but will pass to his personal representative. Equity will, however, perfect the gift by compelling the personal representative to complete the transfer: see, for example, *Re Mead* [1880] (gift of negotiable instrument); *Birch v Treasury Solicitor* [1951] (gift of money in deposit account); and *Sen v Headley* [1991] (gift of donor's house).

A fourth condition could be added to the three conditions above, namely that the property must be capable of forming the subject matter of a valid death bed gift. Until the case of *Sen v Headley* [1991] it was considered that land could not form the subject of a valid donation. However, the Court of Appeal held that the handing over of the title deeds of unregistered land constituted the granting of dominion to the donee. This raises the question whether delivery of the land certificate would suffice should the situation arise with registered land.

There are conflicting cases as to whether stocks and shares can be the subject of a valid death bed gift, e.g. *Moore v Moore* [1874] regarding railway stock, *Re Weston* [1902] regarding building society shares. However, in *Staniland v Wilmott* [1852] it was held that there could be a valid death bed gift of shares in a public company.

(c) Enforcement under the doctrine of proprietary estoppel

If a property owner (O) by his words or conduct represents to another person (P) that P is entitled to an interest in the property, thereby inducing P to act to his detriment, O is *estopped* in equity from denying the truth of the representation.

Estoppel has been invoked in cases where a landowner has made an incomplete transfer of an interest in land and the transferee has relied to his detriment on the belief that the transfer is effective. In such circumstances, equity will compel the owner to transfer the property or do whatever else is necessary to give effect to the transferee's interest: see *Dillwyn v Llewellyn* [1862] and *Pascoe v Turner* [1979].

Two recent House of Lords cases illustrate the doctrine

▶ YEOMAN'S ROW MANAGEMENT LTD v COBBE [2008]

Basic facts

The claimant, Mr Cobbe, a property developer, entered an oral 'agreement in principle' with a director of Yeoman's to the effect that if he succeeded in obtaining planning permission to develop land belonging to Yeoman's, the company would sell the land to him for £12 million.

Mr Cobbe was aware that the oral agreement to sell the land was unenforceable (for lack of compliance with the formality requirement under s2(1) Law of Property (Miscellaneous Provisions) Act 1979) and that a number of important terms remained to be agreed. Nevertheless, he spent much time and money in securing planning permission before Yeoman's withdrew from the original oral agreement.

In the case before the House of Lords, Yeoman's were appealing against the decision of the Court of Appeal that a proprietary estoppel arose in favour of Mr Cobbe for the enforcement of the oral agreement.

The House of Lords allowed the appeal. Cobbe had taken a commercial risk on the basis of an agreement which he knew could not be enforced. Lord Scott stated that, in his opinion, for a claim in proprietary estoppel to succeed, there had to be a clear assurance of a right to an interest in land and this was not fulfilled by an oral agreement to purchase property with important terms to be negotiated in the future. At best, the only expectation Mr Cobbe had was that there would be further negotiations leading to a formal contract.

Lord Scott also stated that 'proprietary estoppel cannot be prayed in aid in order to render enforceable an agreement that statute has declared to be void'. However, in this respect, it should be noted that this was a commercial case and the parties were experienced in business and both knew that neither was legally bound by the agreement. There is a distinction with cases in a domestic or family context such as the House of Lords case *Thorner v Major* [2009] considered below, in which Lord Neuberger said 'I do not consider that section 2 (of the Law of Property (Miscellaneous Provisions) Act 1979) has any impact on an estoppel claim without any contractual connection.'

▶ THORNTON v MAJOR [2009]

Basic facts

Peter Thorner's will made in 1997 left the residue of his estate (which included Steart Farm, Cheddar) to his cousin's son, David Thorner (the appellant). However, due to a dispute with one of the pecuniary legatees, Peter subsequently destroyed his will, intending to make another, but died intestate in 2005. This meant that under the intestacy rules, his estate passed to Peter's sisters, as his closest next-of-kin.

David Thorner had worked on Peter's farm from 1976 until Peter's death in 2005. By 1985 he was working up to eighteen hours a day, seven days a week on his father's farm and Steart Farm, with Steart Farm taking up more than half his time and for no payment in the hope that he would inherit the farm. Although there was no express assurance to this effect, the expectation arose from various remarks and hints by Peter, notably the handing over to David in 1990 of a bonus notice relating to two assurance policies on Peter's life, worth £20,000, which Peter said would be enough to cover his death duties.

In the case before the House of Lords, David Thorner was appealing against a decision of the Court of Appeal that he was not entitled to Peter's farm on the basis of proprietary estoppel.

The issues for the House of Lords related to (1) how specific the assurance by the owner had to be; and (2) whether the claim could succeed when the property, which was the subject of the assurance, had varied in extent since the representations were made (as was the case with Steart Farm).

The House of Lords held that to establish a proprietary estoppel, the claimant must show (a) that the owner's assurance or conduct regarding the property were sufficiently clear; (b) that the assurances or conduct would lead the claimant reasonably to rely on them, i.e. in the words of Lord Hoffman, they were 'understood as intended to be taken seriously'; and (c) that having acted to his detriment in reliance on the assurance, it would be unconscionable to deny the claimant a remedy.

In the present case, the House of Lords held that it was clear from the context of the parties' dealings and conduct over the years that it was reasonable for David to believe that he would inherit the farm, and that it would be unconscionable to deny him a right to the farm as it existed at the time of Peter's death although this was not the same in extent as at the time of the representations.

For further comment on Proprietary Estoppel, see Chapter 7 – Trusts of the Family Home.

You should now be confident that you would be able to tick all of the boxes on the checklist at the beginning of this chapter. To check your knowledge of Constitution of a trust why not visit the companion website and take the Multiple Choice Question test. Check your understanding of the terms and vocabulary used in this chapter with the flashcard glossary.

5

Resulting trusts

Distinguish between an express trust and resulting trust

What is the theoretical basis of resulting trusts?

What is a presumed resulting trust?

When does the presumption of advancement apply?

Which Act will abolish the presumption of advancement?

When does an automatic resulting trust arise?

What is the rule in *Shephard v Cartwright*?

Can evidence of illegal conduct be relied on to rebut a presumption?

Distinguish between *Tinsley v Milligan* and *Tribe v Tribe*

What is a *Quistclose* trust?

What happens to a surplus left after the dissolution of an unincorporated association?

RESULTING TRUSTS

In certain situations, trusts are capable of arising without having been specifically declared by a settlor. Such trusts may either be resulting or constructive. Both types of trusts are accorded statutory recognition in s 53(2) of the Law of Property Act (LPA) 1925, which provides that they need not comply with the same formalities as express trusts.

NATURE AND TYPES OF RESULTING TRUSTS

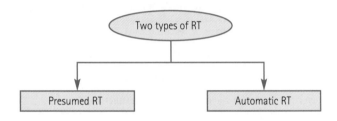

A resulting trust (unlike an express trust) is not deliberately created by the settlor. In *Vandervell Trusts (No 2)* [1974], Megarry J identified two main types of resulting trust:

Presumed resulting trusts: which 1. arise where there is a voluntary transfer of property or purchase in the name of another. For example, if A transfers property into B's name and B gives no consideration (ie it is a voluntary transfer), then there is a presumption against a gift. There is a rebuttable presumption that B holds the property on resulting trust for A. This is presumed to be A's intention.

A — voluntary transfer → B (the legal owner)

                             holds on presumed resulting trust for

                          ↓

                      A (the beneficial owner)

Automatic resulting trusts: which 2. arise in a variety of situations, eg where an express trust fails, the trustees will hold the trust fund on resulting trust for the settlor or his estate. Thus if the settlor is deceased, the trustees will hold the fund on automatic resulting trust for the residuary beneficiary under the sett-lor's will, or if none, for the settlor's statutory next-of-kin under the intestacy rules. Similarly, if the settlor failed to dispose of the entire beneficial interest in an express trust, the trustees will hold the interest on resulting trust for the settlor. The trust fund is said to 'result back' to the settlor.

THE SIGNIFICANCE OF INTENTION IN RELATION TO RESULTING TRUSTS

Resulting trusts have traditionally been imposed on the basis of the *presump-tion* that in undertaking the transfer, A did not *intend* B to take beneficially. In this connection, it was pointed out by Potter LJ in *Twinsectra v Yardley* [1999] that:

> ... whereas express trusts are fundamentally dependent on the sett-lor's intention to create a trust, the role of intention in resulting trusts is a negative one, the essential question being whether or not the provider intended to benefit the recipient and not whether he or she intended to create a trust.

1 Presumed resulting trusts: which arise where there is a voluntary transfer of property or a purchase in the name of another; and
2 automatic resulting trusts: which arise in situations where there is a vacuum in beneficial ownership and 'do not depend on any intentions or presump-tions' – *per* Megarry VC in *Re Vandervell* [1974].

Recently, the view has been expressed that *both* types of resulting trust (not only the presumed resulting trust) depend on the implied intention of the settlor, ie if the settlor thought that an express trust would fail, he would intend the property to return to him – per Lord Browne-Wilkinson in *Westdeutsche Landesbank Girozentrale v Islington LBC* [1996].

PRESUMED RESULTING TRUSTS
Voluntary transfer of property

Where A transfers *personal property* owned by him to B for no consideration, a resulting trust for A is presumed unless B proves that A intended an outright gift to him: see *Standing v Bowring* [1885]; *Re Vinogradoff* [1935]; *Re Muller* [1953]; and *Thavorn v BCCI* [1985].

Before 1925, a resulting trust was also presumed in the case of a voluntary conveyance of *real property*. The position has now been made uncertain by the provision in s 60(3) of the LPA 1925 that, 'in a voluntary conveyance, a resulting trust for the grantor shall not be implied, merely by reason that the property is not expressed to be for the use or benefit of the grantee'.

Some writers suggest that the effect of s 60(3) is that, on a voluntary conveyance of land, a resulting trust will no longer be presumed but will only be imposed if there is evidence that this was the grantor's intention: see, for example, Snell, Pettitt, Chambers and the Law Commission's 1999 Consultation Paper on *Illegal Transactions*. Others maintain that s 60(3) does not preclude a resulting trust from being presumed on general equitable principles. See, for example, Hanbury and Martin's *Modern Equity*; Parker and Mellows' *The Modern Law of Trusts*.

The above view has now been accepted by the courts – see *Khan v Ali* [2002] and *Lohia v Lohia* [2001].

Purchase in another's name

Personal property: Where A purchases *personal property* in B's name, there is a presumed resulting trust in A's favour: see *Fowkes v Pascoe* [1875]; *Shephard v Cartwright* [1955]; *Crane v Davis* [1981]; and *Abrahams v Trustee in Bankruptcy of Abrahams* [1999].

Real property: Where A provides the money for the purchase of *real property* (whether freehold or leasehold) and directs that it should be conveyed or assigned to B or put in B's name, B is presumed to hold it on a resulting trust for A: see *Dyer v Dyer* [1788] and *Gross v French* [1975].

Contributions: A resulting trust may arise where A and B both contribute towards purchasing property. In particular:

- If A and B contribute towards the purchase of property which is conveyed to B, B holds the legal title on resulting trust for A proportionate to his contribution: see *Bull v Bull* [1955]; *Dewar v Dewar* [1975]; *Sekhon v Alissa* [1989]; *Tinsley v Milligan* [1993]; and *Garvin-Mack v Garvin-Mack* [1993].

- If A and B contribute unequally towards property which is put in their joint names, there will be a presumed resulting trust with each party's equitable interest being proportionate to his contribution: see *Springette v Defoe* [1992] and *Tagoe v Layea* [1993].

- If property is purchased in A's name by means of a mortgage and the liability for paying off the mortgage falls on A and B, a resulting trust will be presumed in B's favour in proportion to his liability: see *Moate v Moate* [1948] and *Cowcher v Cowcher* [1972].

- A resulting trust will not, however, arise where B's contribution to property purchased in A's name is merely intended as a loan. See *Re Sharpe* [1980] and *Clark v Manjot* [1998].

Both the presumption of a resulting trust following a voluntary transfer or purchase in another's name may be rebutted by the donee adducing evidence to prove that a gift was intended by the donor. Furthermore, there is a counter-presumption, the presumption of advancement which applies in certain relationships between the donor and donee.

THE PRESUMPTION OF ADVANCEMENT

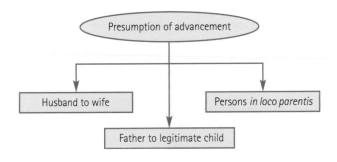

Where A transfers property to B or purchases property in B's name, in circumstances where the presumption of advancement applies, A will be deemed to have intended to make an outright gift to B, unless there is evidence of a contrary intention. This presumption arises in three contexts:

(a) *Husband to wife:* The operation of this presumption where a husband transfers property to his wife or purchases property in her name is illustrated by cases like *Re Eykyn's Trusts* [1877]; *Thornley v Thornley* [1893]; *Gascoigne v*

Gascoigne [1918]; and *Tinker v Tinker* [1970]. This presumption has, however, never been extended to a man's mistress: see *Soar v Foster* [1858]; *Diwell v Farnes* [1959]; and *Garvin-Mack v Garvin-Mack* [1993]. Moreover, the presumption does not arise where property is purchased or transferred into a husband's name by his wife. See *Heseltine v Heseltine* [1975] and *Abrahams v Trustees of the Property of Abrahams* [1999].

In recent decades, wives have become considerably less economically dependent on their husbands than they were when the presumption was conceived. In recognition of this, it has been suggested in *Silver v Silver* [1958] and *Pettitt v Pettitt* [1970] that, although the wife's presumption has not been dispensed with, it ought to be accorded less weight than it was in bygone years.

(b) *Father to legitimate child:* The relationship between a father and his legitimate child has long given rise to a presumption of advancement: see *Lord Grey v Lady Grey* [1677]; *Crabb v Crabb* [1834]; *Re Roberts* [1946]; and *Shephard v Cartwright* [1955]. Note, however, *McGrath v Wallis* [1995] which suggests that the courts are now considerably less inclined to rely on this presumption than they were in the past.

There is no corresponding presumption as between mother and child (see *Re De Visme* [1863]; *Bennet v Bennet* [1879]; and *Ward v Snelling* [1994]); though it was stated in *Bennet* that 'in the case of a mother ... it is easier to prove a gift ... very little evidence beyond the gift is wanted, there being very little motive required to induce a mother to make a gift to her child'.

(c) *Persons in loco parentis:* Where A assumes the position of B's lawful father, A is said to be *in loco parentis*: see *Ex p Pye* [1811]. If A transfers property to B or purchases property in B's name, a presumption of advancement will arise in B's favour: see *Ebrand v Dancer* [1680] (grandfather–grandchild); *Re Paradise Motor Co* [1968] (stepfather–stepson); and *Beckford v Beckford* [1774] (father–illegitimate child).

ABOLITION OF PRESUMPTION OF ADVANCEMENT

Following recommendations by the Law Commission, the presumption of advancement is to be abolished by s199 of the Equality Act 2010. At the time of writing, the section has not yet been brought into force.

Section 199 will remove the presumption of advancement for all transactions which take place after its enactment. Therefore, the old law relating to the presumption of advancement will still apply to transactions which take place before that date.

REBUTTING THE PRESUMPTIONS

Where A transfers property to B or purchases property in B's name, the onus of rebutting the presumption of resulting trust rests with B. He may do so either:

- by proving that the relationship between the parties is one which raises a presumption of advancement in B's favour; or

- by giving evidence of the acts or declarations of either party or of other circumstances which indicate that A wished to confer a beneficial interest on B. Such evidence was found to exist in cases like *Fowkes v Pascoe* [1875]; *Standing v Bowring* [1885]; *Ward v Snelling* [1994]; and *Bradbury v Hoolin* [1998].

Conversely, where A transfers property to B or purchases property in B's name and the operative presumption is of advancement, the onus is on A to rebut this presumption and that he did not intend to confer a beneficial interest on B. Again, this may be done by evidence relating to acts and declarations of the parties or the circumstances surrounding the transfer. Cases in which this presumption was rebutted include *Lord Grey v Lady Grey* [1677]; *Scawin v Scawin* [1841]; *Warren v Gurney* [1944]; *Marshall v Crutwell* [1875]; *Simpson v Simpson* [1992]; and *McGrath v Wallis* [1995].

The rules in *Shephard v Cartwright*

Where the evidence adduced to rebut either presumption consists of acts or declarations, the case of *Shephard v Cartwright* [1955] lays down two rules, namely that:

1 acts/declarations made *before* or *at the time of* the transfer or purchase are admissible either *for* or *against* the maker; while
2 acts/declarations made *after* the transfer or purchase has been concluded are admissible in evidence only *against* the maker.

Evidence of illegal conduct

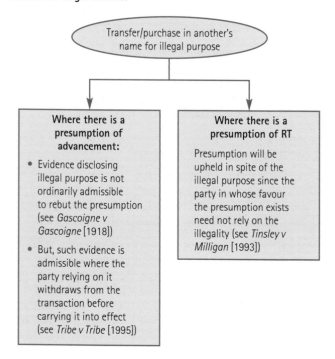

Where, in furtherance of some illegal purpose, A purchases property in B's name or transfers property to B, the 'reliance principle' comes into play. The effect of this principle depends on whether the purchase or transfer is one which gives rise to the presumption of advancement or of resulting trust.

(a) The presumption of advancement

Where A transfers property to B (who happens to be his wife or child) in pursuance of an illegal purpose (for example, to defraud a third party), A can only rebut the presumption of advancement in B's favour by relying on evidence of the illegal purpose. Cases such as *Gascoigne v Gascoigne* [1918]; *Re Emery's Investment* [1959]; *Chettiar v Chettiar* [1962]; and *Tinker v Tinker* [1970] have decided that A will not be allowed to adduce evidence of this illegal purpose and, in effect, will not be able to claim the property beneficially.

The Court of Appeal, however, held in *Tribe v Tribe* [1995] that a father who transferred shares to his son in order to escape liability under impending litigation could rely on this evidence to rebut the presumption of advancement where he withdrew from the illegal purpose before it was carried into effect. This was affirmed *per obiter* by Nourse LJ in *Eeles v Williams* [1998].

(b) The presumption of resulting trust

Where A has purchased property in B's name or transferred property to B (who is not his wife or child), it was held in *Tinsley v Milligan* [1993] that the fact that this was done in pursuance of an illegal purpose will not deprive A of his beneficial interest. This is because a presumption of resulting trust arises in A's favour which means that he need not adduce any evidence and so has no need to rely on the illegal purpose to establish his entitlement. See also *Silverwood v Silverwood* [1997]; *Lowson v Combes* [1998]; and *Eeles v Williams* [1998].

> ### ▶ TINSLEY v MILLIGAN [1994]
>
> #### Basic facts
> Stella Tinsley and Kathleen Milligan were lovers. They jointly purchased a home but legal title was registered in Tinsley's name alone, in order to perpetrate a fraud. Relations between the couple later soured, and Milligan claimed a share by way of resulting trust, but was met with an *ex turpi causa* defence.
>
> The House held in Milligan's favour by a 3–2 majority. Her resulting trust claim was not defeated by her fraud, since the resulting trust arose by presumption, and she did not need to rely on her fraud.
>
> #### Relevance
> The fraudulent enterprise here had been carried into effect. Reading this case along with *Tribe v Tribe* [1995], it appears that where there is trust applied, the transferor of legal title can assert his or her beneficial interest whether or not the fraudulent enterprise has been carried into effect. In effect, changing the 'He who comes to equity must come with clean hands' maxim to 'if he who comes to equity can keep his dirty hands in his pocket he will succeed'.

> It was clear that the position would have been different if the couple had been husband and wife and the house purchased in the wife's name only. In such a case, because of the presumption of advancement, the fraudulent motive would mean that the husband would not be allowed to enforce his interest in the property.

When the presumption of advancement applies, the burden of proof is on the donor of the property to rebut the presumption, ie to adduce evidence to show that a gift was not intended. In contrast, in a resulting trust, it is for the donee to rebut the presumption and prove that a gift was intended. The implications of this are most marked when the transaction was entered into for illegal reasons as is illustrated above.

The fact that A can assert his beneficial interest in property which he puts in B's name where there is a presumption of resulting trust but not where there is a presumption of advancement has led to some criticism of the reliance principle by academic commentators like Martin and Penner, as well as in cases such as *Silverwood v Silverwood* [1997] (Nourse LJ) and *Tribe v Tribe* (Judge Weekes). Nourse LJ declared, for instance, that:

> ... it is not easy to understand or to see any public or other policy or advantage behind a rule which regulates a claimant's right to recover solely according to whether the transfer is to his child or wife ... on the one hand or his brother, grandchild or anyone else on the other.

Similar sentiments were expressed in the 1999 Law Commission Consultation Paper on *Illegal Transactions*, which states that such arbitrariness is difficult to defend and offers a powerful argument for reform in this area.

The Law Commission in its Report No. 320 – The illegality defence – has recommended that courts should have a statutory discretion as to whether a claimant can rely on his legal rights which would apply to a limited class of trusts, for example: trusts created in order to conceal beneficial ownership for a criminal purpose, whether or not the criminal purpose was acted upon, or whether it was the beneficiary or trustee who intended to use the trust to conceal the real ownership. The statutory discretion would also apply to a trust which already existed but continued in order to allow the concealment of the real ownership, and would apply even where the parties did not realise that the concealment was criminal.

The Law Commission report lists factors which would be taken into account by a court when exercising the statutory discretion. These factors include the conduct and intention of all relevant parties, the value of the equitable interest at stake, the effect of allowing the claim, and whether refusing the claim would act as a deterrent.

Summary	
1 Circumstances in which RTs will be presumed:	
(a) voluntary transfer of personalty (b) voluntary transfer of realty (c) purchase in another's name (realty/personalty)	Yes Uncertain (s 60(3) of the LPA 1925) Yes
2 Presumption of RT yields to presumption of advancement in favour of: (a) wife of transferor/purchaser (b) legitimate child where transferor/purchaser is the father (c) person in respect of whom transferor stands in loco parentis	
3 Both presumptions may be rebutted by evidence of contrary intention But note: ■ where the evidence relied on discloses an illegal purpose, it is inadmissible to rebut presumption of advancement ■ where a claim is founded on the presumption of RT, evidence of illegality has no bearing on the claim	

AUTOMATIC RESULTING TRUSTS

For summary, see table on page 84.

A classic illustration of the automatic resulting trust is found in *Vandervell v IRC* and the subsequent case *Re Vandervell Trusts (No 2)* already considered in Chapter 3 regarding statutory formality s 53(1)(c) Law of Property Act 1925.

▶ Re VANDERVELL No. 2

Basic facts
Case following *Vandervell v IRC*. Mr Vandervell still wished to get the company stock into the hands of the trust company. He had the trust company exercise the option, and buy the company shares for a nominal sum.

The trustees then wrote to the Revenue stating that they now held the company shares on trust for Vandervell's children. Vandervell then had dividends declared on the company shares amounting to about a million pounds.

When Vandervell died, the executors of his estate claimed that the dividends on these shares did not belong to the children's trusts, they belonged to the estate. The reason, they argued, was that Vandervell held the option to purchase the shares on resulting trust, so when the option was exercised the trust company held the shares on resulting trust for him, along with the subsequent dividends.

The executors failed in their claim. The court reasoned that when the trust company exercised the option to purchase the shares, with the full approval of Vandervell – who was still the beneficial owner of the option – this completed the express trust that Vandervell had failed to set up the first time around.

Relevance
When Vandervell created a trust of the shares with the trust company as trustee, did he not dispose of his equitable interest? Previously he held on a resulting trust, subsequently he held nothing. We must therefore conclude that Vandervell's disposal of his interest in the shares was not a disposition, and did not require writing under s 53(1)c.

Also per Megarry J in the Chancery division, his lordship divided resulting trusts between '*automatic*' and '*presumed*' resulting trusts.

As Lord Diplock declared in *Vandervell v IRC* [1967], 'equity abhors a beneficial vacuum'. Accordingly, where S transfers property to T under a trust which leaves some or all of the beneficial interest undisposed of, equity automatically fills the vacuum by requiring T to hold the outstanding equitable interest on a resulting trust for S. The main contexts in which such resulting trusts arise are as follows:

1 *Where property passes to T under an express trust which is not effectively declared*: See *Re Keen* [1937] and *Re Vandervell Trusts (No 2)* [1974].

2   *Where an express trust fails because it is subject to a condition which is not fulfilled*: As in *Re Ames' Settlement* [1946].

3   *Where a trust fails to dispose of the whole beneficial interest*: Such as where S gives Blackacre to T on trust for B for life without stating what will happen when B dies. This is often due to bad drafting and, as Harman LJ remarked in *Re Cochrane* [1955], 'a resulting trust is the last resort to which the law has recourse when the draftsman has made a blunder.'

4   *The position where a surplus is left in the trust fund after its purpose has been fulfilled*: In such an event, unless it is established that the settlor/testator intended the trustee to retain the surplus, two possibilities emerge from the decided cases:

   ● In one line of cases, the courts have held that the beneficiaries were not entitled to the whole fund absolutely but only to so much of it as was needed for the specified purpose so that, once the purpose is fulfilled, there will be a resulting trust of the surplus. See *Re Sanderson's Trust* [1851] (trust fund for upkeep of testator's imbecile brother) and *Re the Trust of the Abbott Fund* [1900] (trust fund for the upkeep of two deaf and dumb women). After the deaths of the beneficiaries, in both cases there was a resulting trust of the surplus in their respective funds.

   ● The opposite conclusion was reached in *Re Andrew's Trust* [1905] (trust fund to educate children of deceased clergymen) and *Re Osoba* [1979] (trust of testator's residuary estate to educate his daughter up to university level). In these cases, the court regarded the specified purpose as no more than the motive for the gift and held that the respective beneficiaries were absolutely entitled to the trust fund and could claim the surplus after they had completed their education. This reasoning was adopted in *Davis v Hardwick* [1999]. Here, the people of a village raised a trust fund to enable a child born in the village to undergo pioneering liver transplant surgery and there was a substantial surplus after treatment was completed. It was held that the beneficiary was entitled to the fund absolutely and not only to so much of it as was required for his treatment.

5   *The position where an unincorporated association ceases to exist*: Where this occurs, the association's surplus funds are sometimes dealt with by imposing a resulting trust in favour of the contributors: see, for example, *Re Printers*

and Transferrers Society [1899]; *Re Hobourn Aero Components etc Fund* [1946]; *Davis v Richards and Wallington Industries* [1990]; and *Air Jamaica v Charlton* [1999].

In other cases, however, the courts have favoured a contractual approach. The substance of this approach is that the constitution or other body of rules of an incorporated association constitutes a contract which binds all its members and it is this contract which should determine what will happen to the association's surplus funds in the event of dissolution. This approach was adopted with varying results in a host of cases, such as *Cunnack v Edwards* [1896]; *Re West Sussex Constabulary's Widows, Children and Benevolent Fund Trusts* [1971]; *Re Sick and Funeral Society of St John's Sunday School, Golcar* [1973]; *Re Bucks Constabulary Friendly Society (No 2)* [1979]; *Re GKN Bolts and Nuts Club* [1982]; and *Hanchett-Stamford v AG* [2009].

6 *The position where money is made available for a stated purpose but can no longer be applied for that purpose*: It emerges from the cases of *Barclays Bank v Quistclose Investments* [1970]; *Carreras Rothman v Freeman Mathews Treasure* [1985]; and *Re EVTR* [1987] that this will give rise to a resulting trust. The effect of this '*Quistclose*-type' resulting trust is that the party into whose hands the money was paid will be obliged to hold it on trust for the party who made the money available in the first place. However, where such a payment is made without being required to be set apart and applied for a particular purpose, it will not be subject to a *Quistclose*-type trust. See *Guardian Ocean Cargoes v Banco do Brasil* [1994].

7 *The position where money is paid for a purpose which turns out to be ultra vires*: In the *Westdeutsche* case, a bank paid money to a local authority (LA) under an interest swap agreement which was subsequently declared *ultra vires*.

▶ BARCLAY'S BANK v QUISTCLOSE INVESTMENTS [1970]

Basic facts

Quistclose lent money to RollsRazor (RR) to declare a dividend on its shares. The money was held in a separate bank account at Barclays Bank and provided expressly for that purpose. The loan was made to prevent RR becoming insolvent.

In the event, RR did become insolvent, and never paid the dividend, and Barclay's Bank sought to retain the money to set off against RR's overdraft on the basis that the loan should have become part of RR's general assets, and available to pay off creditors in order of priority. Quistclose sought to recover the sum loaned to RR from Barclays Bank.

The House of Lords held that as there was an express trust between Q and RR, the beneficial interest in the money was therefore not the property of RR at all, and not available to its other creditors. Arguments were advanced that the loan was held in a separate account, and that the loan was to carry out a specific purpose of Q, not RR.

As the bank knew about the original reason for the loan and had agreed to keep it separate, the money was held by Barclays Bank on Resulting Trust for Quistclose.

Relevance

Money lent for a specific purpose creates an Automatic Resulting Trust in favour of the lender upon default of that purpose.

Against this, it has to be noted that the usual principles of insolvency law do not allow an insolvent company to favour one creditor over another.

Nevertheless, as a matter of policy, it can be argued that lending money to a company to protect it from bankruptcy is a laudable objective, and that the law should allow a lender to make such a loan with a degree of protection.

See also *Twinsectra Ltd v Yardley* [2002] in which the claimant, Twinsectra Ltd, a finance company, lent £1 million to Yardley for the purpose of buying land. The money was paid into a client account of Yardley's solicitor, who undertook not to release the money to Yardley except in accordance with the loan conditions. The money was released in breach of this undertaking and used by Yardley to pay off a debt. When Yardley failed to repay the debt, it was held by the House of Lords that the loan money had been impressed with a *Quistclose* trust because it had been paid subject to an undertaking that it would only be used for a specific purpose.

The *Quistclose* principle has been extended over the years. For example, *Re Kayford* [1975] is an example of a *Quistclose*-type trust where the protected creditors were the debtor's customers (rather than lenders).

The Court of Appeal found the LA liable to make restitution of these payments which were made for no consideration not only at law but also in equity; and held that, even though the legal title to the money had passed to the LA, equitable title remained in the bank. In effect, the LA held the money on resulting trust for the bank.

The decision was, however, overturned by the House of Lords which held that the payments made by the bank under the void transaction were recoverable at law as money had and received, but not held on resulting trust by the recipient LA. In his leading judgment, Lord Browne-Wilkinson restated the traditional, conscience-based role of the trust in English law.

Automatic resulting trusts

Summary	
1 Express trust not effectively declared	Property held on resulting trust for settlor
2 Failure of express trust because stipulated condition is not fulfilled	Property held on resulting trust for settlor
3 Failure of express trust to dispose of entire beneficial interest	Undisposed interest held on resulting trust for settlor
4 Surplus left after trust purpose has been accomplished	Three possible outcomes: ■ trustee takes surplus ■ resulting trust of surplus for settlor/contributors ■ gift treated as absolute with surplus passing to intended beneficiaries

5 Surplus left after dissolution of an unincorporated association	Two possible outcomes: ■ resulting trust of surplus for all the members in proportion to their contributions ■ distribution determined by the terms of the contract between those who were members at the time of dissolution
6 Money advanced for a purpose but can no longer be applied for that purpose	*Quistclose*-type resulting trust in favour of party who advanced the money
7 Money paid out in connection with a purpose/scheme which turns out to be ultra vires	HoL decided by a majority in *Westdeutsche* that this is a common law matter

You should now be confident that you would be able to tick all of the boxes on the checklist at the beginning of this chapter. To check your knowledge of Resulting trusts why not visit the companion website and take the Multiple Choice Question test. Check your understanding of the terms and vocabulary used in this chapter with the flashcard glossary.

6

Constructive trusts

How does a constructive trust arise?

Distinguish between a remedial and an institutional constructive trust

Give three examples of the categories of traditional constructive trusts

What is meant by a fiduciary?

When will a fiduciary be liable as constructive trustee?

When is a stranger liable as constructive trustee?

What is the test of dishonesty when dishonest assistance in a breach of trust is alleged?

What is meant by 'recipient liability'?

What is a mutual will?

When might it be relevant to know whether a secret trust is a constructive trust?

CONSTRUCTIVE TRUSTS

THE GENERAL NATURE OF CONSTRUCTIVE TRUSTS

As explained by Edmund-Davies LJ in *Carl Zeiss Stiftung v Smith (No 2)* [1969]:

> 'English law has no clear cut all embracing definition of the constructive trust . . . Its boundaries have been left perhaps deliberately vague so as not to restrict the court by technicalities in deciding what the justice of a particular case may require.'

This is not entirely surprising given that the constructive trust is the residual category of trust which according to Hanbury and Martin 'is called into play where a court desires to impose a trust and no other suitable category exists'.

They arise by operation of law without regard to the intentions of the parties.

INSTITUTIONAL CONSTRUCTIVE TRUST VS NEW MODEL REMEDIAL CONSTRUCTIVE TRUST

In English law the constructive trust has traditionally operated in a number of quite well-defined situations and served to vindicate pre-existing proprietary rights. The constructive trust comes into being when the facts which trigger the operation of law occur.

This contrasts with other common law jurisdictions where the boundaries of the traditional constructive trust have been extended to provide an equitable remedy against a party who has been unjustly enriched. In these circumstances the unjustly enriched party is required to return the property to the claimant.

English law seemed to be developing a version of the new model remedial constructive trust in the 1970s and 1980s. The basis of the imposition of such a trust was held to be that 'justice and good conscience require it' (*per* Lord Denning in *Hussey v Palmer* [1972]). A body of case law developed in relation to disputes between spouses/cohabitees over family property: *Cooke v Head* [1972] and *Eves v Eves* [1975].

Another area in which the constructive trust was deployed in novel circumstances was in the area of the contractual licence: *Binions v Evans* [1972]. Such developments met with academic and judicial criticism based on the unduly subjective nature of the application of fairness and justice, and also because of the threat posed to third parties who might be adversely affected by the imposition of a constructive trust.

Subsequently the courts have been reluctant to extend the boundaries of the new form of constructive trust and have preferred to develop more settled principles.

■ Family home: a common intention between the parties to the effect that the claimant should have a beneficial interest in the property must be established. The judgment of Lord Bridge in *Lloyds Bank plc v Rosset* [1991] has been particularly influential.

■ Contractual licence: the courts have seen a return to orthodoxy in *Ashburn Anstalt v Arnold* [1989].

▶ LLOYD'S BANK v ROSSET [1991]

Basic facts

Mr and Mrs Rosset purchased a semi-derelict farmhouse for £57,000. Mrs Rosset understood that the entire purchase money was to come out of a family trust fund, the trustees of which insisted that the house be purchased in the husband's sole name (this appears to have been the only reason for the legal title being vested in Mr Rosset alone). The house required renovation, and it was intended that this should be a joint venture.

During this period Mrs Rosset spent a lot of time at the house, working with the builders, assisting her husband in planning the renovation and decoration of the house and undertaking numerous other tasks. Unbeknown to Mrs Rosset, Mr Rosset obtained an overdraft of £18,000 from Lloyds Bank, secured over the property. He later defaulted on the repayments, and the bank sought possession. Mrs Rosset claimed a beneficial interest in the property, binding the bank by virtue of her actual occupation, as an overriding interest under the Land Registration Act 1925, s 70(1)(g).

Mrs Rossett's claim failed against the mortgagee, because the House did not accept that her conduct allowed there to be inferred an agreement that she was to have a beneficial share in the property.

Her financial contributions had been small, and her domestic contributions no more than anyone would anticipate on moving into a new home.

Relevance

Doubtful that anything less than direct contributions to purchase/ mortgage will justify inference needed to create a constructive trust.

As Lord Bridge said, the obligations of shared occupancy are not the same as the obligations of shared proprietorship. According to Lord Bridge, for a constructive trust to be raised, the claimant would have to show one of two things:

1 there was an express agreement that he or she was getting a share in the property, albeit vague and dimly remembered, or
2 the agreement would have to be evidenced by 'direct financial contributions'.

For the time being the acceptance of the new model remedial constructive trust into English law seems to have been halted by Lord Browne-Wilkinson's judgment in the *Westdeutsche* case (1996), where he stated the traditional principles of trusts: 'Equity operates on the conscience of the owner of the legal interest. In the case of a [constructive] trust the conscience of the legal owner requires him to carry out the purposes ... which the law imposes on him by reason of his unconscionable conduct.' The House of Lords by a majority of 3:2 declined to impose a constructive trust on monies held by the local authority under an *ultra vires* contract on the basis of unjust enrichment.

The argument, however, continues.

TRADITIONAL CONSTRUCTIVE TRUSTS

Long before the new model approach was conceived, constructive trusts were traditionally recognised in a variety of contexts. Some of these contexts are dealt with below.

CONSTRUCTIVE TRUSTS IN THE CONTEXT OF FIDUCIARY RELATIONSHIPS

Equity has long sought to ensure that a fiduciary does not allow his interests to conflict with his duty: see *Bray v Ford* [1896].

It has been observed in cases like *Re Coomber* [1911] and *English v Dedham Vale Properties* [1978] that fiduciary relationships are many and varied and new types are capable of arising from time to time. As explained in *Reading v Attorney-General* [1951], such a relationship exists whenever one party entrusts another with a job to perform. Its key feature is that one party (the principal) reposes confidence in another (the fiduciary). Elaborating on this, Millett LJ stated in *Bristol and West Building Society v Mothew* [1996] that:

> '. . . a fiduciary is someone who has undertaken to act for or on behalf of another in a particular manner in circumstances which give rise to a relationship of trust and confidence. The distinguishing obligation of a fiduciary is the obligation of loyalty. The principal is entitled to the single-minded loyalty of his [fiduciary].'

A fiduciary will be liable as a constructive trustee in the following circumstances:

1 *Where he receives remuneration to which he is not entitled*: This will be the case where he either:

- makes unauthorised payments to himself or accepts unauthorised payments out of his principal's funds; or

- appropriates to himself payments received from third parties to which the principal is entitled: see *Sugden v Crossland* [1856]; *Erlanger v New Sombrero Phosphate* [1878]; *Williams v Barton* [1927]; *Re Macadam* [1945]; and *Guinness v Saunders* [1990].

2 *Where he enters into a transaction on his own behalf which he should have done on his principal's behalf*: This is exemplified by:

- The rule in *Keech v Sandford* [1726]: this case established that where trust property includes a leasehold interest, the trustee is bound on the expiry of the term to seek a renewal on behalf of the trust. If he renews the lease (or acquires the leasehold reversion) for himself, he will be obliged to hold it on constructive trust for the beneficiaries: see *Keech v Sandford* and *Protheroe v Protheroe* [1968].

- This rule has been extended to other fiduciaries, including personal representatives, agents and partners: see, for example, *Re Biss* [1903].

- The decision in *Regal (Hastings) v Gulliver* [1942]: this case re-affirmed in a different context the principle in *Keech v Sandford*. R Ltd wished to lease two cinemas through a subsidiary, A Ltd. To facilitate the grant of the leases, directors of R Ltd, without authorisation from the shareholders, paid for £3,000 shares in A Ltd. When R Ltd was sold they profited personally from their stake in A Ltd. It was held that they must account as constructive trustees of these profits to the new owners of R Ltd: see also *Industrial Development Consultants v Cooley* [1980]; but note the more flexible approach adopted in Commonwealth cases like *Peso Silver Mines v Cropper* [1966] (Canada) and *Queensland Mines v Hudson* [1978] (Australia).

3 *Where he uses confidential information for his own ends*: The position in this regard is well illustrated by *Boardman v Phipps* [1967], where B, a solicitor to a trust, and TP, one of the beneficiaries, utilised information and opportunities which came their way through their connection with the trust to take control of a company in which the trust had a sizeable shareholding. It was held that they were liable as constructive trustees for the profits which they had made in the process.

In *Crown Dilmun Ltd v Sutton and another* [2004], a duty to account had arisen when the defendant acquired confidential information on behalf of the claimant and utilised this information for his benefit in order to deprive the claimant of an opportunity to make a profit on a property transaction.

The position is, however, different when one party (A) is in a fiduciary relationship with another (B) and as a result of A's breach of his fiduciary duty, a third party (C), who does not stand in a fiduciary position to B, acquires a business opportunity. The Court of Appeal held in *Satnam Investments Ltd v Dunlop Heywood Ltd* [1998] that, in such an event, C will not be liable to B as a constructive trustee.

4 **EXAM ISSUE**: CONTRAST THE TWO CASES – *Lister v Stubbs* and *AG Hong Kong v Reid*. Where a fiduciary receives a bribe: The Court of Appeal decided in *Lister v Stubbs* [1890] that, where a fiduciary accepts a bribe, he does not hold it as a constructive trustee. The relationship is rather one of creditor and debtor. As such, his aggrieved principal will have a personal claim emanating from the fiduciary's liability to account for the amount received but not a

proprietary claim against him, i.e. the employer could not trace into the profitable investments which Stubbs had made with the bribe money. The decision has received much criticism and was expressly disapproved by the Privy Council in *AG for Hong Kong v Reid* [1993] where bribes had been accepted by Reid and invested in three properties in New Zealand. Reid was deemed to hold the property on constructive trust and consequently a proprietary claim was available. Lord Templeman stated: 'As soon as the bribe was received it should have been paid ... to the person who suffered from the breach of duty. Equity considered as done that which ought to have been done. As soon as the bribe was received, whether in cash or in kind, the false fiduciary held the bribe on a constructive trust for the person injured.'

Such an interpretation, although desirable, is not without its difficulties, e.g. if the false fiduciary is insolvent, should his unsecured creditors be deprived of their right to a share in the proceeds of the property purchased by the bribe?

In *Daraydan Holdings v Solland Interiors* [2004], the High Court applied the principle in *Reid* and decided that a fiduciary who received a bribe or a secret commission became a constructive trustee for his principal and was accountable for the sums received.

This differentiation between a personal liability to account and the imposition of a constructive trust is significant at two levels:

● in the event of the fiduciary's insolvency, the principal would be accorded priority over the fiduciary's other creditors in respect of property held on constructive trust but not funds/property which is subject to a liability to account; and

● in the event of an increase in value of the property in the fiduciary's hands, the principal would be able to claim the benefit of the increase if held on constructive trust but not if there is only a personal liability to account.

See also *Dyson Technology Ltd v Curtis* [2010] considered later under dishonest assistance.

In *Sinclair Investments (UK) Ltd v Versailles Trade Finance Ltd* [2011] the Court of Appeal held that a beneficiary was only entitled to a personal claim and could not claim a proprietary interest in respect of assets purchased by a fiduciary in breach of trusts with funds which were not beneficially owned by the beneficiary or derived from an opportunity or right beneficially owned by the beneficiary.

5 *Loans for general purposes obtained by fraud*: The creation of a loan constitutes a chose in action in favour of the lender. The borrower acquires both legal and equitable interests in the property. In *Shalson and others v Russo and others* [2003], it was decided that where the creditor rescinds the loan by virtue of the fraudulent representation of the borrower, the beneficial interest in the loan re-vests in the creditor who acquires an equitable interest by way of a constructive trust.

Strangers as Constructive trustees

■ *Bona fide* purchaser for value ■ Innocent volunteer ■ Person dealing with property as agent	Not liable as constructive trustee
■ Trustee *de son tort* ■ Accessory assisting in breach of trust ■ Person guilty of knowing receipt	Liable as constructive trustee

A trustee (or other fiduciary) who improperly allows property or funds entrusted to him to fall into the hands of strangers will be liable for any loss occasioned to the beneficiaries. Where the trustee cannot make good the loss, it has to be determined whether the stranger will be liable as a constructive trustee.

The stranger will not be liable as a constructive trustee:

■ where he acquires trust property as a *bona fide* purchaser of the legal estate for value without notice: see *Pilcher v Rawlins* [1872];

■ where he receives trust property as an innocent volunteer: in such an event, the beneficiary can trace the property into the hands of the recipient if it still exists in some traceable form. However, he is not in a fiduciary position vis à vis the beneficiary and will not be liable as a constructive trustee if the property passes out of his hands without his being aware of the trust: see *Re Diplock* [1948]; *Re Montagu's ST* [1987]; *Agip (Africa) v Jackson* [1992]; and *Westdeutsche Landesbank v Islington LBC* [1996];

■ where he is an agent of the trustee: trustees often delegate aspects of their responsibilities to agents like solicitors, stockbrokers and valuers and entrust trust property to such agents. The general rule in this regard is that an agent of the trust who acted honestly in the performance of his agency will not be liable for losses occasioned to the trust estate: see *Lee v Sankey* [1873]; *Barnes v Addy* [1874]; *Mara v Browne* [1896]; and *Williams-Ashman v Price and Williams* [1942].

SITUATIONS IN WHICH A STRANGER WILL BE A CONSTRUCTIVE TRUSTEE

A stranger who deals with trust property (including an agent) will be liable as a constructive trustee in three contexts, notably:

■ where he is a *trustee de son tort*;

■ where he is an *accessory*; or

■ where he is a *recipient* of such property.

(1) *The trustee de son tort*

Cases like *Mara v Browne* [1896] establish that, if a person who is not a trustee and has no authority from the trustee becomes involved in administering the trust estate, he is a trustee *de son tort*. This makes him liable as a constructive trustee for the trust assets as well as for any loss occasioned by him. See also *James v Williams* [1999] where a constructive trust was imposed on a defendant who had administered an intestate estate without a grant and had acted throughout as if he was solely entitled to the estate.

(2) *Accessory liability* (now referred to as Dishonest Assistance in a Breach of Trust)

Cases such as *Soar v Ashwell* [1893] and *Barnes v Addy* established the principle that a stranger who dishonestly assists a trustee (or other fiduciary) in a breach of duty would be liable as a constructive trustee for any loss occasioned by the breach.

In some instances, the stranger's role as an accessory will involve the receipt of property in an administrative capacity which he then deals with or disposes of in accordance with the fraudulent designs of the trustee/fiduciary (as happened in *Agip (Africa) v Jackson* [1992]).

In other instances, the accessory's involvement will arise in circumstances which do not entail his receipt of property from the trustee. See, for example, *Eaves v Hickson* [1861] and Lord Browne-Wilkinson's judgment in the *Westdeutsche* case. In such circumstances, his liability to account will invariably be personal rather than proprietary. This has prompted various commentators (Pettit, Martin, Birks, etc) to suggest that it is a misnomer to categorise him as a constructive trustee. This view was echoed by Potter LJ in *Twinsectra v Yardley* [1999].

According to Peter Gibson J in *Baden Delvaux v Société Générale* [1983], accessory liability involves the following four elements:

(a) *The existence of a trust or other fiduciary relationship.*

(b) *The existence of a dishonest and fraudulent design on the part of the trustee/ fiduciary:* Particular emphasis was laid on this requirement in cases like *Soar v Ashwell* and *Barnes v Addy*. It was, however, held in *Royal Brunei Airlines v Tan* [1995] that this is not an essential requirement.

(c) *Assistance by the stranger:* In order for a stranger to be liable as an accessory, there must be some measure of participation on his part. Thus, for instance, in *Brinks Ltd v Abu-Saleh* [1995], where a wife had simply accompanied her husband on foreign holidays which he had used as a cover for money laundering operations, this did not render her liable.

(d) *Guilty knowledge on the part of the stranger:* In this context, the courts have recognised that knowledge has many shades of meaning. Peter Gibson J, himself, identified five possible categories of knowledge which could be ascribed to a stranger.

His first three categories ((1) direct knowledge; (2) deliberately averting one's eyes to the obvious; and (3) wilful failure to make inquiries) are indicative of conscious impropriety or dishonesty on a stranger's part and categories (2) and (3) are thus treated on the same footing as actual knowledge. It has never been in doubt that these three categories of knowledge will render a stranger liable.

His last two categories (knowledge of circumstances which would (4) indicate the facts to a reasonable man; or (5) put an honest and reasonable man on inquiry) are generally regarded as tending more towards lack of care rather than dishonesty. Over the years, there has been a marked divergence of judicial opinion on the issue of whether a stranger could be affixed with liability on the strength of such negligence-based knowledge.

This issue was settled by the Privy Council in the *Royal Brunei Airlines v Tan* [1995] case, where Lord Nicholls conducted a detailed survey of the principles governing accessory liability and concluded that:

■ dishonesty is a necessary ingredient of accessory liability;

■ dishonesty is for the most part to be equated with conscious impropriety and carelessness is not dishonesty;

■ 'knowingly' is best avoided as a defining ingredient in determining the liability of an accessory and the *Baden* scale of knowledge is best forgotten.

In *Twinsectra Ltd v Yardley* [2002] UKHL 12, the House of Lords by a majority equated the test for dishonesty with the criminal law definition of the expression laid down in *R v Ghosh* [1982] QB 1053. This involves a combined (objective/subjective) standard to the effect that the claimant is required to prove that the defendant is:

■ dishonest by the ordinary standards of reasonable and honest people (objective); and

■ that he himself realised that his conduct was dishonest by those standards (subjective).

In *Barlow Clowes International Ltd (in Liquidation) v Eurotrust International Ltd* [2006], the Privy Council moved back to a purely objective test for dishonesty. Thus the defendant would not be able to rely on his own moral code to absolve him from liability. Lord Hoffmann stated 'If by ordinary standards, a defendant's mental state would be characterised as dishonest, it is irrelevant that the defendant judges by different standards.'

In *Abou-Rahmah v Abacha* [2006], which involved an action against a Nigerian registered bank for dishonest assistance in a fraudulent scheme, the Court of Appeal appeared to endorse the Privy Council decision in *Barlow Clowes* and described the test for dishonesty 'as predominantly objective'. Per Arden LJ: 'It is sufficient if the defendant knows of the elements of the transaction which make it dishonest according to normally accepted standards of behaviour.'

In *Starglade Properties Ltd v Roland Nash* [2010] the Court of Appeal held that the relevant standard of honesty is the ordinary standard of honest behaviour and just as the subjective understanding of the person involved as to whether his conduct was dishonest or not is irrelevant, it is also irrelevant that there may be a body of opinion which regards the ordinary standard of honest behaviour as being set too high. Ultimately, it was for the court to determine what that standard was and to apply it to the facts of the case.

> ▶ **DYSON TECHNOLOGY LTD v CURTIS [2010]**

Basic facts

A former employee of the claimant company was in breach of fiduciary duty for receiving bribes from tooling manufacturers over a number of years as an incentive to place the claimant company's contracts with them.

The bribes had been paid into the accounts of two of his wife's companies, who knew or suspected that she was assisting in a misappropriation of money.

Regarding her liability for dishonest assistance, it was held that it was sufficient if a defendant knew of the elements of a transaction which made it dishonest according to normally accepted standards of behaviour and it was not necessary for the defendant to be aware of the precise nature of the underlying breach or to know that the money was held on trust or what was meant by a trust. The wife was liable for dishonest assistance and it was open to the claimants to pursue a proprietary claim against her.

(3) *Recipient liability*

A stranger who receives trust property for his own benefit does not ordinarily take free from the trust unless he is a *bona fide* purchaser for value without notice. He may thus be compelled to restore any property in his hands to the beneficiary, once he is affixed with notice of the trust, whether actual or constructive.

If the property is no longer in the recipient's hands, the beneficiary may still be able to proceed against him on the footing that he is under a personal liability to account in much the same way as an accessory. This has traditionally been characterised as liability for '*knowing receipt*' which points to the fact that a recipient would be affixed with liability only if he had some knowledge of the fact that the transfer was in breach of trust. There has, however, been some controversy regarding the degree of cognisance required.

On the one hand, in *Re Montagu's ST* [1987], Megarry VC insisted that a recipient would only be liable if he had actual knowledge of the *Baden* (1)–(3) categories.

A contrary view was taken in the earlier case of *Karak Rubber v Burden (No 2)* [1972] where Brightman J held that a recipient would be liable if he had actual or constructive notice (the latter being akin to knowledge within the *Baden* (4)–(5) categories). More recently, in cases like *Agip (Africa) v Jackson* [1992] and *El Ajou v Dollar Holdings* [1994], Millett LJ considered that a doctrine analogous to the doctrine of constructive notice had a place in the receipt cases which suggested to him that actual knowledge (within categories (1)–(3)) was not a pre-condition for recipient liability.

A recent trend has been to recharacterise liability for knowing receipt as liability for unjust enrichment upon which a *restitutionary claim* can be founded. This is evident, for instance, in the New Zealand case of *Powell v Thompson* [1991] as well as in the *El Ajou* and *Royal Brunei* cases. In *Powell*, Thomas J indicated that, while accessory liability is based on unconscionable conduct, recipient liability is based on unjust enrichment. A similar distinction was drawn in *Royal Brunei* by Lord Nicholls, who stated that 'recipient liability is restitution based, accessory liability is not'. In similar vein, Millett LJ observed in *El Ajou* that:

> [Recipient liability] is the counterpart in equity of the common law action for money had and received. Both can be classified as receipt based restitutionary claims.

If this reasoning is accepted, it follows that the mere fact of receipt will ordinarily give rise to personal liability, even if the recipient is an innocent volunteer who is devoid of any knowledge or notice.

The movement away from knowing receipt as strict liability regardless of fault which is implicit in the restitutionary approach has not met with universal approval. This is borne out by Lord Browne-Wilkinson's endorsement of the traditional approach in the *Westdeutsche* case, where he declared that unless a third party recipient 'has the requisite degree of knowledge he is not personally liable to account as trustee'.

It remains to be seen which of these positions will ultimately prevail.

In *BCCI v Akindele* [2000] 3 WLR 1423, the Court of Appeal took the view that owing to a single test for dishonesty for accessory liability, likewise there ought to be a single test of knowledge for knowing receipt cases. The recipient's state of knowledge must be such as to make it unconscionable for him to retain the subject matter of receipt. The test of unconscionablility is imprecise and involves subjective knowledge or dishonesty on the part of the defendant.

OTHER CATEGORIES OF CONSTRUCTIVE TRUST
These include:

The common intention constructive trust
See ownership of the family home in Chapter 7.

Secret trusts
See Chapter 3 regarding fully and half secret trusts. It is not entirely settled whether secret trusts (in particular half secret trusts) are constructive trusts or express trusts.

Mutual wills
Mutual wills typically arise where a husband and wife *agree* to make wills in *similar or identical terms*, eg leaving their property to the other and on the death of the survivor, the property to pass to a named beneficiary such as their child. They also *agree not to revoke their wills.* See *Re Oldham* [1925], *Re Goodchild* [1997].

The problem arises when one of the spouses dies having kept to the agreement but the survivor makes a new will. (A person can always revoke their will and make a new will. Indeed s 18 Wills Act 1837 provides that a marriage revokes a person's will.) However, in such a situation, the law may impose a constructive trust on the survivor to respect the agreement. There is dicta to the effect that the trust comes into existence on the death of the first spouse and crystallises upon the death of the second spouse – *Re Cleaver* [1981]. It is sometimes referred to as a floating trust.

In *Re Dale (deceased)* [1994] it was held that mutual wills can arise whether or not the survivor takes a benefit from the will of the first to die as where a husband and wife agree to leave nothing to each other but to leave everything to a third party.

▶ Re WALTERS (DECEASED) – ALSO KNOWN AS WALTERS v OLINS [2008]

Basic facts

In 1998, the appellant, Mr Walter and his wife (now deceased) made codicils drafted by the respondent Mr Olins (a solicitor and one of the appellant's grandsons) in which they agreed to leave their residuary estate to each other absolutely and following the death of both of them, their property would go to their grandchildren. There was ample evidence that they had agreed that after the first of them died, they did not want the survivor to suffer pressure to change the testamentary arrangements, and that Olins should implement their intention that their respective wills could only be changed by agreement during their joint lives and could not be changed by the survivor.

When Mrs Walters died, Mr Walter inherited her estate but subsequently quarreled with Olins and did not want to leave his estate as agreed with his wife.

It was held by the Court of Appeal that the intentions of Mr Walters and his wife were sufficiently expressed in the contract to lay the foundations for the equitable obligations that were binding immediately on the conscience of Mr Walters, as the survivor, in relation to the deceased's estate and were not postponed to take effect only after the death of Mr Walters.

In *Charles v Fraser* [2010] the High Court held that, having regard to the terms of identical wills of two elderly sisters in which each bequeathed the residue of their estate to trustees to divide the proceeds into forty equal parts to be divided between certain named beneficiaries, together with the close relationship of the sisters and other surrounding circumstances, there was clear evidence of an irrevocable agreement between the two sisters to establish valid mutual wills.

If it is not clear from the terms of the will as to which property is subject to the trust, there is a problem. Clearly property which the survivor received from the estate of the first to die in accordance with the agreement is subject to the trust. However, does the trust also attach to property which the survivor personally owned at that time? *Re Hagger* [1930] would suggest that it does. Further, does the trust attach to all the property which the survivor owned at the time of his/her death? This could be unfair where for example the survivor won the lottery, or remarried and acquired new dependants. This issue remains undecided.

It may now be possible for the beneficiary to pursue his claim in contract, ie enforcing the contract between the testators under the Contracts (Rights of Third Parties) Act 1999 provided the contract was made after 11th May 2000 when the Act came into effect.

You should now be confident that you would be able to tick all of the boxes on the checklist at the beginning of this chapter. To check your knowledge of Constructive trusts why not visit the companion website and take the Multiple Choice Question test. Check your understanding of the terms and vocabulary used in this chapter with the flashcard glossary.

Trusts of the family home

7

What is meant by 'Equity follows the law' in this context?

What must the non-legal owner, who claims she has a
beneficial interest in the home, prove in order to establish:

an express trust;

a resulting trust;

an express common intention constructive trust;

an inferred common intention constructive trust?

How will her beneficial interest be quantified in each of
the above cases?

What is meant by proprietary estoppel?

What remedies are available under proprietary estoppel?

Who may rely on s 37 of the Matrimonial Proceedings &
Property Act 1970?

What is wrong with the current law regarding trusts of
the family home?

What recommendations for reform have been made by
the Law Commission?

TRUSTS OF THE FAMILY HOME

Where a married or unmarried couple have set up home together, events such as the breakdown of the relationship or bankruptcy of either party may give rise to a dispute over their respective interests in the family home.

If the married couple are pursuing matrimonial proceedings, eg judicial separation, divorce, then the dispute will be settled under the Matrimonial Causes Act 1973 which empowers the court to make whatever order is just and practicable regarding the property of both spouses without being bound by strict rules of property law. If the dispute is between same sex registered partnerships, then the Civil Partnership Act 2004, gives the court similar powers to those under the Matrimonial Causes Act 1973.

Where the dispute falls outside the ambit of the Matrimonial Causes Act 1973 or the Civil Partnership Act 2004 (for example where it is between one spouse and a third party, or where the cohabitants are unmarried), the beneficial interests in the family home are determined under the general rules of property law. As Lord Diplock explained in *Gissing v Gissing* [1971], the operative principles in such cases are derived from the law of trusts.

THE RELEVANCE OF LEGAL TITLE

JOINT LEGAL OWNERS

A statutory trust of land arises automatically under the Trusts of Land (Appointment of Trustees) Act 1996 when two or more persons are joint legal owners of land. Since April 1998, where land is to vest in joint registered proprietors, Land Registry forms now make provision for the joint legal owners to execute a declaration of trust so as to determine their beneficial interests in the property. 'No one doubts that such an express declaration is conclusive unless varied by subsequent agreement or affected by proprietary estoppel' *per* Baroness Hale in *Stack v Dowden* [2007] citing *Goodman v Gallant* [1986].

When there is no express declaration of the beneficial interests in the deed (as in *Stack v Dowden*), eg because the transfer occurred before 1998, the majority of the House of Lords in that case agreed that there is a presumption that the joint legal owners are owners of the equitable interest in the home equally, ie 'equity follows the law'. This presumption will only be rebutted in unusual circumstances such as existed in *Stack v Dowden*. Although the parties (unmarried) had lived together for 20 years and had four children, they had kept their financial affairs rigidly separate and Ms Dowden had made a considerably greater financial contribution to the purchase of the home. 'This is all strongly indicative that they did not intend their shares, even in the property which was put into both their names, to be equal ... Before the Court of Appeal, Ms Dowden contended for a 65% share and in my view she has made good her case for that,' *per* Baroness Hale.

In *Fowler v Barron* [2008], the Court of Appeal applied the decision in *Stack v Dowden* that where property was conveyed in joint names, the starting point was joint beneficial ownership and the burden was on the party who sought to dispute that. Even though Miss Fowler did not make any direct contributions to the purchase price, she had looked after the children and Mr Barron was unable to show why the beneficial interest in the house should be different to the legal title.

▶ KERNOTT v JONES [2010]

Basic facts

In 1985, the parties, Ms Jones and Mr Kernott, who had a young child, purchased a property in joint names for £30,000. Ms Jones contributed £6,000 and the balance of the purchase price was raised by mortgage.

In 1986, a second child was born, and an extension was built and paid for largely by Mr Kernott, raising the value of the house to £44,000. The couple shared household bills, including the mortgage payments.

The parties separated in 1993 and Ms Jones and the children remained in the house. It was agreed at that time that their beneficial interests in the property were equal.

In 1996, Mr Kernott bought a property for £57,000 raising the deposit by cashing in a life policy which he and Ms Jones owned, the proceeds of which they divided equally.

In May 2006, more than 12 years after their separation, during which time Ms Jones had assumed sole responsibility for the maintenance of the children and the outgoings on the house, Mr Kernott sought payment of a half share in the house which the couple had purchased together.

The trial judge held that Ms Jones' investment towards the purchase of the property and since separation meant that she was entitled to a greater share and the beneficial interests were fixed at 90% for Ms Jones and 10% for Mr Kernott.

The Court of Appeal allowed Mr Kernott's appeal that the parties' beneficial interests were equal. Following *Stack v Dowden*, the conveyance into joint names created joint beneficial interests and there was no evidence from which a common intention to vary the equal beneficial interests could be inferred, the passage of time being insufficient to do so.

At the time of writing, Ms Jones' appeal is before the Supreme Court.

LEGAL ESTATE IN THE NAME OF ONE SPOUSE/COHABITANT

Where the legal estate to the home is in the name of one spouse or cohabitant, then *prima facie per Stack v Dowden*, the legal owner should be presumed to be the sole owner of the equitable interest in the home. However, this is a presumption and the other party may seek to claim a share in the beneficial interest in various ways by relying on

- an express trust

- a resulting trust

- a constructive trust

- proprietary estoppel

- s 37 Matrimonial Proceedings & Property Act 1970.

The second stage of the process is to quantify the claimant's interest in the home.

Express trust

Land Registry forms do not make provision for the beneficial interests to be declared if the legal title is in the name of one party only. However, the legal owner is free to make an express declaration of trust in favour of the other party. If this is alleged by the claimant, then it must be shown that the declaration of trust of land was evidenced in writing and signed by the legal owner in accordance with s 53(1) (b) Law of Property Act 1925 (see statutory formalities – Chapter 3).

The beneficial interest will be quantified in accordance with the terms of the express declaration.

The imposition of a resulting trust

Following *Stack v Dowden*, the resulting trust (sometimes referred to as a purchase money resulting trust/presumed resulting trust) is out of favour in the context of the family home (as opposed to commercial property or property purchased as an investment), and the inferred common intention constructive trust is preferred. The following should be read with that in mind.

Traditionally, where the property is in the male partner's name but the female partner contributes directly to the purchase price, a resulting trust will be presumed in her favour in proportion to her contribution.

If the male partner contributes directly to the purchase price but the property is put in the name of the female partner, the position will depend on whether she is his wife or cohabitant.

- in the case of a cohabitant, a resulting trust is presumed in favour of the contributing male partner; but

- in the case of a wife, there is a weak presumption of advancement and the onus is thus on the husband to prove that he did not intend an outright gift to her.

Direct contributions giving rise to a resulting trust refer to payment of the price, or the deposit, or acceptance of legal liability for the mortgage, or a contribution by qualification for a discount. See *Cowcher v Cowcher* [1972], *Curley v Parkes* [2004] and *Springette v Defoe* [1992].

The beneficial interest under a resulting trust is quantified arithmetically, proportionate to the direct contribution to the purchase price – *Arogundade v Arogundade* [2005].

The imposition of a constructive trust

Constructive trusts have been imposed in disputes relating to the family home since the early 1970s when the two landmark cases of *Pettitt v Pettitt* [1970] and *Gissing v Gissing* [1971] were decided.

These cases established that where the legal title to the home is vested in one partner, a claim by the other to a beneficial share under a constructive trust will succeed if: (1) there was a common intention that the claimant will acquire an interest in the home; and (2) the claimant has relied on this to his or her detriment.

In a later line of cases, which included *Cooke v Head* [1972]; *Eves v Eves* [1975]; and *Hall v Hall* [1982], Lord Denning's attachment to the new model approach led him to treat the constructive trust in this sphere purely as a discretionary formula for adjusting the property rights of spouses and co-habitees in order to achieve a fair and just solution between them.

The new model approach lost momentum after Lord Denning relinquished judicial office and the courts have now reverted to the more orthodox principles laid down in *Gissing* and *Pettitt*, in cases such as *Burns v Burns* [1984]; *Midland Bank v Dobson* [1986]; *Grant v Edwards* [1986]; and most decisively by the House of Lords in *Lloyds Bank v Rosset* [1991]. These principles as articulated in *Rosset* have been reiterated and adopted in a host of subsequent cases such as *Hammond v Mitchell* [1991]; *Springette v Defoe* [1992]; *Midland Bank v Cooke* [1995]; and *Clough v Kiley* [1996].

The notable effect of this reversion to orthodoxy is that a constructive trust will no longer be imposed on a co-habitee or spouse just because this is perceived to be fair and just, but can only be imposed where the requisite *common intention* and *detrimental reliance* are established.

According to Lord Bridge's analysis in *Lloyds Bank v Rosset,* there are two categories of case.

The Express Common Intention Constructive Trust

There are two essential elements. First there must be evidence of an arrangement or agreement or understanding between the parties (ie evidence of the express common intention) to share the beneficial interest. An excuse as to why the property was conveyed into one party's name may be treated as express evidence of an unspoken understanding between the parties that the claimant was entitled to a beneficial interest in the home – *Eves v Eves* [1975], *Grant v Edwards* [1986] and *Hammond v Mitchell* [1991].

Secondly, there must be an act of detriment by the claimant on the basis of the common intention – termed detrimental reliance. This was described by Nourse LJ in *Grant v Edwards* as 'conduct on which the woman could not reasonably be expected to embark unless she was to have an interest in the home'.

The detrimental reliance may assume various forms:

- contributing towards household expenses: see *Grant v Edwards* [1986];

- supporting the other partner's business ventures which are financed by loans secured by the family home: see *Hammond v Mitchell* [1991];

- contributing financially towards the cost of conversion works on the property: see *Drake v Whipp* [1995];

- contributing in kind to improving the property: see *Eves v Eves* [1975].

Regarding quantification – if the express arrangement/agreement states the beneficial share that the parties are to take, this will apply. Where the arrangement/agreement was silent, then the share will be quantified by the court – see *Oxley v Hiscock* and *Stack v Dowden* below under 'Inferred Common Intention Constructive Trust'.

The Inferred Common Intention Constructive Trust

In this case, there is no evidence of an express agreement/understanding/arrangement, but a common intention is inferred from the **direct contributions** of the claimant to the purchase price of the home, by means of an initial capital payment or payment of mortgage instalments. Thus a common intention to share the beneficial interest will be imputed by the court by direct contributions. In *Lloyds Bank v Rosset*, Lord Bridge said 'it is extremely doubtful whether anything less will do'. However, it has been suggested, eg by Lord Walker in *Stack v Dowden*, that a broader view should be taken – to include **indirect financial contributions**. See also *Le Foe v Le Foe* [2001] in which it was stated that it was an arbitrary allocation of responsibility that one party paid the mortgage, service charges and outgoings, whereas the claimant paid for the day to day domestic expenditure. See also the words of Lord Diplock in *Gissing v*

Gissing – 'it may be no more than a matter of convenience which spouse pays particular household accounts, particularly when both are earning and if the wife goes out to work and devotes part of her earnings or uses her private income to meet the joint expenses of the household which would otherwise be met by the husband, so as to enable him to pay the mortgage instalments out of his monies, this would be consistent with and might be corroborative of an original common intention that she should share in the beneficial interest...'

However, it is clear that **purely domestic contributions** will not give rise to an inferred common intention constructive trust – see *Burns v Burns* [1984].

Regarding quantification, in *Stack v Dowden,* the House of Lords endorsed the approach taken by the court in *Oxley v Hiscock* [2005] that the court should have regard to 'the whole course of dealing between the parties'. However, in doing so, the court should consider what the parties were taken to have intended rather than imposing what the court considered fair. See also *Abbott v Abbott* [2007].

PROPRIETARY ESTOPPEL

This is similar to the express common intention constructive trust and is often founded on the same facts. There are three elements: assurance/representation by the legal owner, detrimental reliance by the claimant and denial of the claimant's rights by the legal owner. Thus the claimant must prove that the owner of the home encouraged or led the claimant to believe that she had enjoyed some right or benefit over the land. In reliance on such assurance, the claimant acted to her detriment. The range of remedies 'to satisfy the equity' are diverse. Examples include the conveyance of the house in *Pascoe v Turner* [1979], the grant of a right of occupancy in *Greasley v Cooke* [1980], the sum of £200,000 in *Jennings v Rice* [2002], i.e. three farms and £110,000 in *Gillett v Holt* [2001]. For further discussion of proprietary estoppel – see Chapter 4 under exceptions to the maxim that equity will not perfect an imperfect gift.

SECTION 37 MATRIMONIAL PROCEEDINGS AND PROPERTY ACT 1970

This applies to improvements made to the family home by married couples. The Act does not apply to unmarried parties.

The section provides that where a husband or wife contribute in money or money's worth to the improvement of real or personal property, he or she shall be treated as having thereby acquired a share or enlarged share in the property.

NEED FOR REFORM AND LAW COMMISSION RECOMMENDATIONS

EXAM ISSUE: Deficiencies in current law and recommendations for reform

There are many deficiencies in the current law – foremost that a cohabitant must rely on property law to establish his or her rights in the family home since there is no legislation allowing the court to exercise its discretion and make property adjustment orders, etc. as there is upon the dissolution of a marriage or civil partnership. The different types of trust which may be relied on in such circumstances each has its limitations: for example an express trust requires compliance with s53(1)(b) LPA 1925, the resulting trust (now out of favour following *Stack v Dowden* [2007] regarding ownership of the family home but still relevant with respect to investment property or commercial property) applies only to direct contributions made towards the purchase price with rights crystallising at the time of purchase and with no recognition given to a cohabitant who did not accept liability for the mortage at the outset but simply assisted the legal owner with mortgage payments. Then there is the fiction of the express common intention constructive trust and the likelihood of lengthy and expensive litigation as the court seeks to determine the common intention of the parties and detrimental reliance, the apparent overlap of this type of constructive trust with proprietary estoppel, and the range of remedies available with proprietary estoppel leading to uncertainty. Then there is the question of whether indirect financial contributions will give rise to an inferred common intention constructive trust as in *Le Foe v Le Foe* [2001] (and dicta in *Stack v Dowden*), but the lack of recognition of purely domestic contributions – *Burns v Burns* [1984].

It is generally considered that legislative intervention is long overdue. The House of Lords case *Stack v Dowden* [2007] itself has raised a number of uncertain issues, some of which are likely to be answered in *Kernott v Jones* [2010] on appeal to the Supreme Court at the time of writing. These issues include:

- ■ Why is there a presumption of shared beneficial ownership in cases of joint legal title?

- ■ Is detriment needed when the presumption of equality of beneficial ownership is challenged by the claimant?

- ■ What are the 'exceptional circumstances' which are required to rebut the presumption of equality?

- ■ Were the circumstances in *Stack v Dowden* so exceptional?

- ■ What is 'imputed intention'?

- ■ Does it apply only when the court is considering quantification of the beneficial interest?

- ■ Should imputing an intention to share ownership be extended to the cohabitant of a home registered in the name of a sole legal owner?

- ■ Is detriment still required in sole legal ownership cases?

The Law Commission has recommended a statutory scheme for cohabitants (ie those who are not married and are not civil partners) *Law Commission Cohabitation: The Financial Consequences of Relationship Breakdown* (Law Com No. 307). The Law Commission favours an opt-out scheme, ie a scheme which will apply to eligible parties unless they decide to opt out of the scheme. Parties would be eligible if they have lived in a joint household for a certain period or they have a child. The Law Commission recommended that this should be between two and five years.

A claim would be considered where the applicant had made a qualifying contribution (financial or otherwise) and as a result had suffered a continuing economic disadvantage or the other party had retained a benefit. Thus the applicant would have to show that she had for example contributed towards the respondent's mortgage payments (whereby he retained a benefit) or for example that she had cared for the couple's children and did not pursue her career which would affect her future earning capacity and pension rights (ie she would suffer a continuing economic disadvantage).

The Law Commission recommends that the court should have wide powers to order transfer of property, or capital payments.

It has been stated that the government is awaiting the results of research on the relatively new scheme for cohabitants in Scotland under the Family Law (Scotland) Act 2006 before proceeding with legislation.

You should now be confident that you would be able to tick all of the boxes on the checklist at the beginning of this chapter. To check your knowledge of Trusts of the family home why not visit the companion website and take the Multiple Choice Question test. Check your understanding of the terms and vocabulary used in this chapter with the flashcard glossary.

Charitable trusts

8

Philanthropic persons often seek to contribute to the well-being of society either:

■ by making donations to voluntary bodies established for charitable purposes; or

■ by giving property or money to trustees of their own choice to be held for purposes which are charitable.

THE SIGNIFICANCE OF CHARITABLE STATUS

The Charity Commission and courts often have to determine whether a trust or voluntary body is charitable. Where a trust is recognised as charitable, it enjoys certain advantages which do not extend to trusts in the private domain. In particular:

■ a private trust fails if its objects are uncertain, whereas a charitable trust is valid even if it does not specify a precise purpose;

■ a private trust will also fail where the settlor's intention cannot be carried out but a charitable trust is much less likely to fail on this account in view of the *cy-pres* doctrine;

■ the perpetuity rules do not apply with the same degree of stringency to charitable trusts as they do to private trusts, ie the rule against perpetual trusts does not apply;

■ charitable trusts enjoy many fiscal advantages over private trusts.

For example, a trading charity is exempt from income tax or corporation tax where either the trade is exercised in the course of carrying out the main purpose of the charitable trust or the work in connection with the trade is carried out by beneficiaries of the charitable trust. A charity is exempt from capital gains tax, and may claim relief (of at least 80%) from payment of non domestic rates on premises which are wholly or mainly used for charitable purposes. A charity also enjoys exemption from the payment of stamp duty on conveyances. Gifts in favour of charity are exempt from inheritance tax and relief is available on 'gift aid' donations.

THE LEGAL POSITION BEFORE THE CHARITIES ACT 2006

The preamble to the Charitable Uses Act 1601 contained a list of purposes regarded as charitable and became the guide to the development of the law on charitable purposes over the next two hundred and ninety years. Charitable purposes were not only those listed in the preamble but those within the 'spirit and intendment' of the preamble. By drawing analogies with the charitable purposes stated in the preamble, new charitable purposes were recognised.

Then in *Commissioners for Special Purposes of Income Tax v Pemsel* [1891], Lord Macnaghten classified existing charitable objects under four heads: for the relief of poverty; for the advancement of education; for the advancement of religion and other purposes beneficial to the community. The 'spirit and intendment' of the preamble continued to influence the development of the law under the fourth head.

In addition to the requirement of a *charitable purpose*, it was also necessary to prove that the trust was for the *public benefit* and that it was *exclusively charitable*. These three requirements remain as will be seen below.

THE CHARITIES ACT 2006

Meaning of 'charity' and 'charitable purposes'

Section 1(1)(a) of the Act specifies that a body or trust is a charity if established for charitable purposes 'only'. This preserves the rule that a body or trust must have objects which are *exclusively charitable*. If it has non-charitable as well as charitable purposes, it is not a charity.

Section 2 of the Act contains the first statutory definition of *charitable purpose*. It is one which is for the *public benefit* and which falls within any of the following thirteen heads of charitable purposes listed in s 2(2).

(a) the prevention or relief of poverty;

(b) the advancement of education;

(c) the advancement of religion;

(d) the advancement of health or the saving of lives;

(e) the advancement of citizenship or community development;

(f) the advancement of the arts, culture, heritage or science;

(g) the advancement of amateur sport;

(h) the advancement of human rights, conflict resolution or reconciliation or the promotion of religious or racial harmony or equality and diversity;

(i) the advancement of environmental protection or improvement;

(j) the relief of those in need by reason of youth, age, ill-health, disability, financial hardship or other disadvantage;

(k) the advancement of animal welfare;

(l) the promotion of the efficiency of the armed forces of the Crown, or the efficiency of the police, fire and rescue services or ambulance services;

(m) any other purposes within subsection (4).

Section 2(4) covers those purposes that are currently recognised as charitable but that do not fall under any of the specific descriptions in paragraphs (a) to (l), as well as allowing the meaning of 'charitable purpose' to be expanded in the future by allowing for the possibility of new charitable purposes to be recognised. This affirms the former approach of reasoning by analogy by reference to decided cases.

Section 3 lays down the second part of the definition of a charity namely the 'public benefit' test. Under the former law there was a presumption that purposes for the relief of poverty, the advancement of education, or the advancement of religion were the public benefit. Section 3(1) now stipulates that each of the listed purposes is required to satisfy the public benefit test. Section 3(2) declares that no presumption will be made to the effect that a purpose satisfies the public element test. Thus, if there is a dispute as to the validity of a charitable purpose, the trustees of the organisation are required positively to establish that the purpose has a real and substantial benefit to society.

THE THIRTEEN HEADS OF CHARITABLE PURPOSES

These are now examined in greater detail. The first three heads are those identified by Lord Macnaghten in *Pemsel* but his fourth category 'other purposes

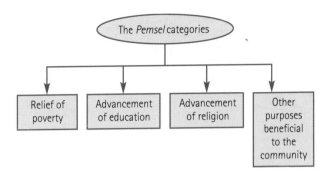

beneficial to the community' has been sub-divided – see (d)-(m) below. It follows that much of the former case law is relevant to the new heads of charitable purposes.

(a) *The relief of poverty*

Poverty, as Evershed MR pointed out in *Re Coulthurst* [1951], is a word of wide and indefinite import. It may range from outright destitution to the relative deprivation of a person who has known better times. As a general guide, he suggests that a person can fairly be regarded as poor if he has to go short in the ordinary acceptance of the word, regard being had to his status in life and so forth.

The clearest indication that the intended purpose is to relieve poverty is where the declaration of trust explicitly refers to poverty or similar words: see, for example, 'needy': *Re Reed* [1893]; *Re Scarisbrick* [1951]; 'indigent': *Weir v Crum-Brown* [1908]; 'limited means': *Re Gardom* [1914]; 'fall[en] on evil days': *Re Young's WT* [1951].

Even where such explicit words are not used, the very nature of a gift may denote that it is intended to relieve poverty: see, for example, *Biscoe v Jackson* [1887] (establishment of soup kitchen); *Re Lucas* [1922] (modest weekly payments to the old). A trust will not, however, qualify as one for the relief of poverty where its benefits are not exclusively reserved for the poor, even if it is framed in terms which suggest that those who are likely to claim the benefits will be poor: see *Re Gwyon* [1930] and *Re Sander's WT* [1954], but contrast the latter case with *Re Niyazi's WT* [1978].

(b) *The advancement of education*

The preamble mentions 'the education ... of orphans' as well as 'the maintenance of schools of learning, free schools and scholars in universities'. The ancient universities and public schools have long enjoyed charitable status which has now been extended to newer universities, colleges and schools: see, for example, *AG v Margaret and Regius Professors in Cambridge* [1682]; *The Case of Christ's College Cambridge* [1757]; and *Re Mariette* [1915].

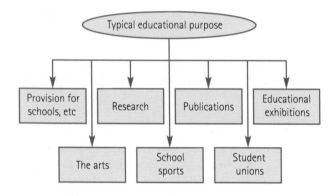

The advancement of education is not restricted to the process of formal learning in a classroom environment. It encompasses a wide range of other activities which, in the words of *McGovern v AG* [1981], contribute to 'the improvement of a useful branch of human knowledge and its public dissemination'.

The following have been held to be charitable under this head:

Research:	See: *Besterman's WT* [1980], where a clear definition of 'research' was given. Contrast the position of Harman J in *Re Shaw's WT* [1957] with that of Wilberforce J in *Re Hopkin's WT* [1964]. Note, also, the conditions laid down by Slade J in *McGovern v AG* [1981]
Educational publications:	*ICLR v AG* (Law Reports); *Re Stanford* [1924] (New English Dictionary)

Educational exhibitions:	*British Museum Trustees v White* [1826]; *Re Lopes* [1931]
Artistic activities:	*Re Shakespeare Memorial Trust* [1923]; *Re Delius* [1957]; *Royal Choral Society v IRC* [1943]. Contrast with *Re Pinion* [1965] where charitable status was refused
Sports in education:	*Re Mariette* [1915]; *Re Dupree's DT* [1945]; *IRC v McMullen* [1981]. Note, however, Vaisey J's remarks in *Dupree* concerning the difficulties in deciding which sports are educational and which are not
Student unions:	To the extent that they promote the general welfare of members and cater for their social, physical and cultural needs, the law treats the unions as charitable: see *Baldry v Feintuck* [1972]; *London Hospital Medical College v IRC* [1976]; *AG v Ross* [1986]; *Webb v O'Doherty* [1991]

EXAM ISSUE: *Politics masquerading as education*: Cases such as *Re Bushnell* [1975]; *McGovern v AG* [1981]; and *Southwood v AG* [1998] have established that a trust or organisation whose purposes are ostensibly educational will not be accorded charitable status where these purposes are meant to further some political agenda, ideology or goal. By the same token, cases such as *Baldry v Feintuck* [1972] and *AG v Ross* [1986] have held that bodies which are considered to be charitable in the educational sphere will be precluded from engaging in political activities or supporting political causes. See, further, the Charity Commission Guidelines on *Political Activities and Campaigning by Charities* (2004) and 'Speaking Out – Guidance on Campaigning and Practical Activities by Charities' (2008).

(c) *The advancement of religion*

Christianity: The charitable purposes enumerated in the CUA 1601 include the repair of churches. In the centuries which have followed, numerous other purposes and organisations associated with Christianity have been recognised as charitable. In the first place, charitable status has been conferred on various Christian denominations and movements: see, for example:

■ *Re Barnes* [1930]; *Re Tonbridge School Chapel (No 2)* [1993]	Church of England
■ *Re Schoales* [1930]; *Re Flinn* [1948]; *Re Hetherington* [1989]	Roman Catholic Church
■ *Re Strickland's WT* [1936]	Baptist Church
■ *Re Nesbitt's WT* [1953]	Unitarians
■ *Holmes v AG* [1981]	Plymouth Brethren
■ *Re Fowler* [1914]	Salvation Army
■ *Thornton v Howe* [1862]; *Re Watson* [1973]; *Funnell v Stewart* [1996]	Obscure sects on the fringes of Christianity

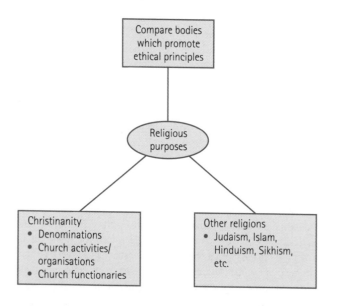

Furthermore, gifts for a wide range of purposes connected with Christianity have also been held to be charitable:

■ Maintenance of the fabric of a church or chapel	*Re King* [1923] stained-glass window; *Re Pardoe* [1906] church bells; *AG v Day* [1900] the gallery; *Re Eighmie* [1935] church cemetery
■ Upkeep of the clergy	*Pember v Inhabitants of Kington* [1639]; *Middleton v Clitheroe* [1798]; *Re Williams* [1927]; *Re Forster* [1939]
■ Preaching of sermons	*Re Parker's Charity* [1863]
■ The saying of masses	*Re Caus* [1934]; *Re Hetherington* [1989]
■ Promoting missionary work abroad	*Re Maguire* [1870]; *Re Clergy Society* [1856]
■ Choral singing in church	*Re Royce* [1940]
■ Prizes for Sunday school	*Re Strickland* [1936]
■ Gifts to religious communities	*Re Banfield* [1968] (except cloistered communities: see *Gilmour v Coats* [1949])

Other ways in which a donor may denote that a gift is meant to promote Christianity are:

■ by stating that it should be applied 'for God's work' (*Re Barker's WT* [1948]) or 'to the service of God' (*Re Darling* [1896]) or using other words to the same effect;

■ by making the gift to a clergyman (for example, a bishop or vicar) in terms which limit the scope of the gift to the donee's religious functions: see *Re Garrard* [1907]; *Re Flinn* [1948]; *Re Rumball* [1956]; *Re Bain* [1930]; *Re Simson* [1946]; and *Re Eastes* [1948].

EXAM ISSUE: Contrast with other cases like *Farley v Westminster Bank* [1939] and *Dunne v Byrne* [1912] which involved gifts to clergymen for purposes that went beyond religion.

The charitable status of non-Christian faiths: In *Thornton v Howe*, Romilly MR observed that the court 'makes no distinction between one sort of religion and another'. This view was echoed in *Neville Estates v Madden* [1962] by Cross J who affirmed that, 'as between religions, the law stands neutral, but it assumes that any religion is better than no religion at all'. He therefore held that a trust for the purpose of building and running a synagogue was a valid trust for the advancement of religion. By the same token, the charitable status of a mosque was judicially recognised in *Birmingham Mosque Trust v Alavi* [1992]. More recently, the charitable status of a Hindu sect was upheld in *Varsani v Jesani* [1998].

At the same time, the Charity Commission have registered as charitable various organisations which propagate non-Christian faiths such as Islam, Hinduism and Sikhism. Note that s 2(3)(a) of the Charities Act 2006 states that 'religion' includes (i) a religion which involves belief in more than one god and (ii) a religion which does not involve belief in a god. It is unclear how (ii) above will effect ethical systems of belief – see below.

In September 2010, the Charity Commission approved the registration of the Druid Network, an unincorporated association as a charity for the advancement of religion.

The Commission was satisfied that druidry as defined by the Druid Network was not simply a philosophy or way of life but had a spiritual reverence and recognition of nature which was regarded as the supreme being or entity (a necessary characteristic of religion for the purposes of English charity law). The Commission was satisfied that the Network fulfilled the requirement of tending directly or indirectly to the moral and spiritual improvement of the public and there was evidence of an identifiable positive and beneficial ethical framework that was capable of having a beneficial impact of the community at large (eg by promoting conservation and preservation of the environment). The public benefit guidance confirms that a 'religion must be a sincere belief system of substance or significance, capable of benefiting society, having a certain level of cogency, coherence, seriousness and importance, as opposed to a self promoting organisation set up to promote one or two persons' and the Commission was satisfied that this requirement was fulfilled.

The status of non-religious bodies which promote ethical principles: It emerges from cases like *Re South Place Ethical Society* [1980] and *United Grand Lodge v Holborn LBC* [1957] that such bodies are not considered to be charitable in the religious sphere, though they might be charitable within another sphere, eg advancement of education.

(d) *The advancement of health or the saving of lives*

Relief of sickness **EXAM ISSUE: Even when patients are expected to pay, still charitable** – see *Re Resch's WT* [1969]	■ **Hospitals:** *Re Smith's WT* [1962]; *Re Resch's WT* [1969]
	■ **Home for nurses in a hospital:** *Re White's WT* [1951]
	■ **Training of nurses:** *RCN v St Marylebone Corp* [1959]
	■ **Medical research:** *Steel v Wellcome Custodian Trustees* [1988]
	■ **Accommodation for patients' relatives:** *Re Dean's WT* [1950]
	■ **Relieving physical or psychological illness or addictions:** *Re Lewis* [1955]; *Re Chaplin* [1933]; *Re Banfield* [1968]

The RNLI and mountain rescue services would be examples of organisations aimed at saving lives.

(e) *The advancement of citizenship or community development*
Section 2(3)(c) of the Charities Act 2006 explains that this head includes 'rural or urban regeneration and the promotion of civil responsibility, volunteering, the voluntary sector or the effectiveness or efficiency of charities.

(f) *The advancement of the arts, culture, heritage or science*
This head overlaps with the advancement of education – see artistic activities above. Other examples include: British Heritage, the National Trust.

(g) *The advancement of amateur sport*
Section 2(3)(d) of the Charities Act 2006 states that 'sport' means 'sports or games which promote health by involving physical or mental skill or exertion'. In the past, mere sport or recreational activities were not in themselves charitable (ie unless part of education or provided in the interests of social welfare under the Recreational Charities Act 1958) – see *Re Nottage* [1895], *IRC v City of Glasgow Police Athletic Association* [1953].

(h) *The advancement of human rights, conflict resolution or reconciliation or the promotion of religious or racial harmony or equality and diversity*
This head encompasses a number of activities including promoting good race relations and combating discrimination on grounds of religion, gender, age, sexual orientation.

(i) *The advancement of environmental protection or improvement*

This would include the protection of wildlife, areas of outstanding natural beauty, combating global warming, research into biodiversity, recycling, energy preservation.

(j) *The relief of those in need by reason of youth, age, ill-health, disability, financial hardship or other disadvantage*

This would include the welfare of the elderly *Re Lucas* [1922]; *Re Robinson* [1951]; *Rowntree MT Housing Association v AG* [1983].

This head would include all existing trusts under the Recreational Charities Act 1958 which has been amended by the Charities Act 2006. The Act provides that the provision of, or assistance in the provision of facilities for recreation or other leisure time occupation shall be charitable if the facilities are provided in the interests of social welfare. The requirement of social welfare is satisfied if the facilities improve the condition of life of persons who have need of the facilities by reason of their youth, age, infirmity or disability, poverty or social and economic circumstances OR if the facilities are available to the members of the public at large, or male, or female members of the public at large. Examples would be the provision of a women's only swimming pool, women's institutes, boys' clubs.

(k) *The advancement of animal welfare*

This would include existing charities such as the RSPCA, animal hospitals, homes for lost dogs.

It may be that the House of Lords decision in *National Anti-vivisection Society v IRC* [1948] would remain. The society failed to gain charitable status mainly because it sought to change the law and as such was regarded as political. See also *Hanchett-Stamford v Att. Gen.* [2008] in which the Performing and Captive Animals Defence League was denied charitable status for the same reason.

(l) *The promotion of the efficiency of the armed forces of the Crown, or of the efficiency of the police, fire and rescue services or ambulance services*

This would include purposes for the defence of the realm, such as protection from air attacks *Re Driffill* [1949]; gift to officers' mess *Re Good* [1905]. Regarding the efficiency of national rescue services – *Re Wokingham Fire Brigade Trusts* [1951].

(m) *Any other purposes within sub-section (4)*

This sub-section provides that purposes which are recognised as charitable will continue to have charitable status even though they are not expressly stated under the heads above. The sub-section also provides for further development by recognising as charitable any purposes that may reasonably be regarded as analogous to purposes under the new heads or to purposes which have been recognised under charity law in the past but which are not expressly stated under the new heads.

An example would include the rehabilitation of ex-offenders.

THE PUBLIC BENEFIT REQUIREMENT

As Farwell J observed in *Re Delany* [1902], 'charity is necessarily altruistic and involves the idea of benefit to others'. This notion of altruism is reflected in the general rule that a trust is not charitable if its intended beneficiaries are those for whom the donor would feel naturally obliged to provide; whereas it will be charitable if it is intended to benefit the wider community or the public at large in some way.

This rule has assumed particular importance in modern times, when many settlors seek to alleviate the heavy burden of personal and corporate taxation by 'enlist[ing] the assistance of the law of charity in private endeavours in order to gain tax benefits', *per* Lord Cross in *Dingle v Turner* [1972].

Section 3(2) of the Charities Act 2006 changes the law by removing the former presumption that trusts under the first three heads of Lord Macnaghten's classification, ie for the relief of poverty, advancement of education and advancement of religion, were for the public benefit. Now all trusts are required to demonstrate (on an annual basis to the Charity Commissioners) the provision of public benefit.

However, s 3(3) of the Charities Act provides that any reference to public benefit in that part of the Act is a reference to public benefit as that term is understood for the purposes of the law relating to charities in England and Wales. In other words, the requirement for public benefit should be in accordance with the definition of public benefit as applied in case law before the Charities Act 2006 came into force.

It is therefore clearly relevant to consider past case law on public benefit in respect of Lord Macnaghten's four categories of charitable purposes before considering the recent guidance on public benefit issued by the Charity Commission.

The poverty exception

Prior to the Act, a trust for the relief of poverty of a small class of persons between whom there was some personal nexus (eg of blood in the case of poor relations, or of contract in the case of poor employees) was upheld despite the lack of public benefit. This was known as the poverty exception and the following are examples.

(It is unclear whether s 3(3) of the Charities Act above means that this poverty exception will still apply.) At the time of writing, this is the subject of a reference by the Attorney General to the newly established Charity Tribunal.

Designated class	Relevant cases
Donor's relations	*Isaac v Defriez* [1754]; *Re Scarisbrick's WT* [1951]; *Re Cohen* [1973]; *Re Segelman* [1995]
Poor employees	*Re Gosling* [1900]; *Gibson v South American Stores* [1950]; *Dingle v Turner* [1972]
Members of a common trade or profession	*Thompson v Thompson* [1844] writers; *Spiller v Maude* [1881] actors
Members of friendly society	*Re Buck* [1896]
Members of donor's club	*Re Young* [1951]

In the light of these cases, Hanbury and Martin have concluded that 'the requirement of public benefit has been reduced in the field of poverty almost to vanishing point'.

Education

The public benefit requirement has been stringently applied in the educational sphere than it is in the field of poverty.

Where the benefits of an educational trust are available not to the public at large but only to the members of a specified class, it will be charitable only if the class forms an appreciable section of the community. According to the test laid down in *Re Compton* [1945], this will be the case if two criteria are met:

- the members of the class must not be numerically negligible; and

- the quality which distinguishes the members of the class from the community at large must not be one which depends on their relationship to a particular individual.

Applying this test, the court held that a trust to educate the descendants of three named persons was not charitable.

EXAM ISSUE: Subsequently, in *Oppenheim v Tobacco Securities Trust* [1951], the House of Lords invoked the *Oppenheim* test as the basis for holding that a trust for the education of the children of employees and former employees of a tobacco company was not charitable. Note, however, the dissenting judgment of Lord MacDermott who drew attention to the difficulties and contradictions which are liable to arise if the test is taken to its logical conclusion. See also the judgment of Lord Cross in *Dingle v Turner* [1972].

Employers have sometimes attempted to avoid the implications of the *Compton* test by creating educational trusts ostensibly for the general public while prevailing on the trustees to utilise the bulk of the trust fund to educate the children of employees. A trust of this nature was recognised as charitable in *Re Koettgen* [1954]. By contrast, a similar type of scheme was denied charitable status in *IRC v Educational Grants Association* [1967]: see also *Caffoor v Income Tax Commissioner Colombo* [1961].

Religion

The operation of the public benefit requirement in the religious sphere has been most vividly illustrated by *Gilmour v Coats* where a gift to an order of cloistered nuns, who had no contact with the outside world, was held not to be charitable.

The position is different where the gift is to a religious body or movement which does not restrict its services or observances to a closed group of members. It has been held, in cases like *Thornton v Howe* [1862]; *Re Watson* [1973]; and *Re Le Cren Clarke* [1995], that such a gift fulfils the public benefit requirement even where the body or movement is an obscure one with very few adherents.

129

❯ GILMOUR v COATS [1949]

Basic facts

A sum of money was to be held on trust for the purposes of a community of cloistered nuns, who devoted their lives to prayer, contemplation, penance and self-sanctification within their convent and engaged in no exterior works.

Held, that the purposes of the priory were not charitable.

Relevance

The element of public benefit is essential to render a purpose charitable in law and this applies equally to religious as to other charities. The benefit of intercessory prayer to the public is not susceptible of legal proof and the court can only act on such proof. Further, the element of edification by example is too vague and intangible to satisfy the test of public benefit.

Other purposes beneficial to the community

The public benefit requirement was central to the validity of trusts which came within the fourth head. According to *Verge v Somerville* [1924], the charitable status of such trusts depends on whether the benefits which they provide are available to the community at large or an appreciable section of the community.

The courts have pronounced on the operation of the public benefit requirement under the fourth head in cases such as:

■ *Williams Trustees v IRC* [1947]: where it was held that a trust for the benefit of Welsh people in London was not charitable since they did not form an appreciable section of the community;

■ *IRC v Baddeley* [1955]: where it was held that a trust which provided a recreational outlet for members/would-be members of the Methodist church in West Ham (among other things) was not charitable since this was not a section of the community but a class within a class.

Although cases like *Goodman v Saltash* [1882] and *Peggs v Lamb* [1993] concluded that trusts for the inhabitants of a defined geographical area are charitable, it was observed by Lord Cross in *Dingle v Turner* that the operation of the public benefit requirement may be problematic where such trusts are concerned; for example, a trust for the ratepayers of the Royal Borough of Kensington may be seen from one perspective as a charitable trust for a section of the community and from another perspective as trust for a fluctuating body of private individuals. Example: a bridge for the exclusive use of 'Methodists' or 'the Welsh population' of an area will not be charitable, even if they form a substantial part of the community.

Finally, as Lord Simmonds emphasised in *Baddeley*, once the benefits of a trust are open to the public or an appreciable section thereof, the trust is deemed to be charitable even if relatively few people take advantage of the benefits. Thus, for instance: 'A bridge which is available for all the public may undoubtedly be a charity and it is indifferent how many people use it.'

The discussion above, despite focussing on the pre-2006 heads, applies equally to the expanded list of 13 heads under s 2 of the Charities Act 2006.

Charity Commission guidance on public benefit

s4 of the Charities Act 2006 requires the Charity Commission to issue guidance on the public benefit requirement and this it has done in Charities and Public Benefit – January 2008, in which it identified the following principles.

Principle 1 – There must be an identifiable benefit or benefits

1a – it must be clear what the benefits are;

1b – the benefits must be related to the aims of the charity;

1c – benefits must be balanced against any detriment or harm.

Principle 2 – Benefit must be to the public, or a section of the public

2a – the beneficiaries must be appropriate to the aims;

2b – where benefit is to a section of the public, the opportunity to benefit must not be unreasonably restricted:

– by *geographical or other restrictions; or*

– *by ability to pay any fees charged.*

2c – people in poverty must not be excluded from the opportunity to benefit;

2d – any private *benefits must be incidental.*

131

These principles have been developed in a number of guidance documents, eg The Advancement of Religion for the Public Benefit – December 2008, Public Benefit and Fee-Charging – December 2008, Analysis of the Law Underpinning Charities and Public Benefit – December 2008.

Some of these principles reflect the decisions in past cases, for example regarding the principle that there must be an identifiable benefit – see *Gilmour v Coats* [1949] – the House of Lords held that the benefits conferred on the public by the prayers of the nuns and the example they set of a spiritual life were too vague to be proved to be of tangible benefit to the public.

The principle that the public benefit must be balanced against any possible detriment is exemplified by *National Anti-Vivisection Society v Inland Revenue Commissioners* [1948] in which the House of Lords held that the benefit to mankind in suppressing vivisection was far outweighed by the detriment to medical research and therefore charitable status was denied.

Regarding the principle that the benefit must be for the public of a sufficient section of the public – this is illustrated by two leading cases *IRC v Baddeley* [1955] and *Williams' Trustee v IRC* [1947]. See also the personal nexus test applied in *Oppenheim v Tobacco Securities Trust Co* [1951] which the Charity Commission has recently stated should be retained although caution and flexibility should be exercised in the application of the test.

THE REQUIREMENT THAT THE TRUST MUST BE EXCLUSIVELY CHARITABLE

A trust that is framed in terms which enable the trustees without being in breach of trust to expend any part of the trust fund on non-charitable purposes is liable to fail on the ground that it is not exclusively charitable. In *Williams Trustees v IRC* [1947], for instance, a trust which was predominantly for valid educational purposes was held not to be exclusively charitable because one of its purposes (namely, promotion of sport and recreation among Welsh people living in London) was not deemed to be charitable: see also *IRC v City of Glasgow Police AA* [1953]; *AG Cayman Island v Even Wahr-Hansen* [2001].

The failure of a charitable trust on this ground is often the result of imprecise drafting. The major difficulty in this regard is the inappropriate use of words like benevolent, deserving, philanthropic, public and worthy which have the same connotation as the concept of charity in ordinary usage but which are considered to be of wider import than charity in the legal sense. Cases such as *Morice v Bishop of Durham* [1805] and *Re Gillingham Bus DF* [1958] have held that the effect of using such words is that the trust will not be exclusively charitable.

The problem is especially acute where the draftsman uses the word charitable in combination with such words of wider import. The guiding principles in such cases may be summarised as follows:

■ Where the connecting word is '**or**', this is ordinarily construed disjunctively which means that the trust will not be regarded as exclusively charitable: see, for example, *Blair v Duncan* [1902] (charitable or public); *Re Diplock* [1948] (charitable or benevolent); *AG v National Provincial Bank* [1924] (charitable or patriotic); and *Houston v Burns* [1918] (public, benevolent or charitable). But, note *Re Bennet* [1920] where a gift 'to charity or other public purpose' was held to be exclusively charitable.

■ Where the connecting word is '**and**', this is ordinarily construed conjunctively so that the word of wider import is drawn into the ambit of the charitable and the trust is, in effect, exclusively charitable: see *Blair v Duncan* [1902] (charitable and public); *Re Sutton* [1885] (charitable and deserving); and *Re Best* [1904] (charitable and benevolent).

The requirement that a trust must be exclusively charitable has been relaxed in the following contexts:

■ where the inclusion of a non-charitable element is designed to facilitate the performance of the trust's charitable purpose: see *Re Coxen* [1948];

■ where the non-charitable element is merely incidental to the charitable purpose which constitutes the basis of the trust: see *IRC v City of Glasgow Police AA* [1953]; *ICLR v AG* [1972]; and *Re Le Cren Clarke* [1995];

■ where the trust is framed in terms which enable the court to sever the part of the trust fund intended for charity from the part intended for non-charitable purposes: see *Salusbury v Denton* [1857];

■ by virtue of the Charitable Trusts (Validation) Act 1954, where a trust is declared for purposes which are partly charitable and partly non-charitable and the instrument creating the trust came into effect before 16th December 1952, the trust will operate as if it were exclusively for the charitable purposes: see *Re Wyke's WT* [1961]; *Re Meade's Trust Deed* [1961]; and *Leahy v AG for New South Wales* [1959].

THE *CY-PRES* DOCTRINE

EXAM ISSUE: The *cy-pres* doctrine

Where a charitable trust is validly declared, circumstances may render it impossible, impracticable or inappropriate to carry out the donor's charitable purpose. In such an event, it is often possible to give effect to the donor's general charitable intention by applying the *cy-pres* doctrine (as near as). The effect of the doctrine is to enable the trust property to be used for some other purpose which resembles the donor's original purpose.

It is a different matter where a trust fails because it does not satisfy any of the requirements for a valid charitable trust. In such a case, the defect cannot be cured by invoking the *cy-pres* doctrine. The doctrine was not relied on, for instance, in *Re Gillingham Bus DF* [1958] and *Re Jenkins' WT* [1966], both of which involved trusts whose purposes were not exclusively charitable.

THE *CY-PRES* DOCTRINE – THE CASE LAW POSITION

Before the Charities Act 1960 was enacted, the doctrine applied:

- *where there was a surplus after a specified charitable purpose had been duly accomplished*: see, for example, *Re King* [1923] where a testator left £1,500 to install a stained glass window in a church. The cost of the window was about £800 and it was held that the balance should be spent on a second window;

- *where it was impossible/impracticable to perform the specified purpose*: in *Biscoe v Jackson* [1887], for instance, there was a legacy of £4,000 to provide a soup kitchen and cottage hospital in Shoreditch. When this proved to be impossible because there was no suitable land in the area, it was held that the fund could be applied *cy-pres* to other purposes: see also *Re Burton's Charity* [1938]; *Re Dominion Student's Hall Trust* [1947]; and *Re Hillier* [1944].

The doctrine was, however, inapplicable where the intended purpose did not represent an efficient use of resources or was outdated or difficult to fulfil or otherwise unsuitable, without being impossible or impracticable. A case in point is *Re Weir's Hospital* [1910], where property which a testator had devised to be used as a hospital was unsuited for this purpose but the court refused to permit the property to be applied *cy-pres* to some other purpose.

A distinction is made in case law between the initial failure of a charitable trust and subsequent failure, ie failure after the trust has been in operation.

INITIAL FAILURE AND THE REQUIREMENT OF GENERAL CHARITABLE INTENT

The courts have established in a long line of cases that, where a charitable gift cannot take effect at the outset due to the *initial failure* of the donor's charitable purpose, the doctrine will only apply if the donor possessed *a general charitable intent*.

Such intent was discernible for instance in *Biscoe v Jackson* where the sum of £4,000, which a testator directed was to be used to set up a soup kitchen/ hospital, was to be taken out of a bequest of £10,000 which he had expressly made to charity. See also *Re Lysaght* [1966] and *Re Woodhams* [1981].

By contrast, the *cy-pres* doctrine is excluded in cases of initial failure, where the donor did not evince a general charitable intent, but rather intended that the gift should be used for the purpose prescribed by him and nothing else. Thus, in *Re White's Trust* [1886], a gift to establish an almshouse for poor tinplate workers failed because no suitable site was available and the fund was insufficient to maintain an almshouse. The *cy-pres* doctrine was held to be inapplicable on the ground that the donor did not intend the gift to be used for any other purpose and a resulting trust arose in favour of the donor's estate. See also *Re Rymer* [1905]; *Re Wilson* [1913]; and *Re Good's WT* [1950].

Gifts to charities which have ceased to exist

Where property is given to a charity which has become defunct at the date of the gift, this will ordinarily be treated as a case of initial failure and the *cy-pres* doctrine will apply only if the donor had a general charitable intent.

In two contexts, however, a gift to a defunct charity will not give rise to initial failure (and will therefore be valid without the need to prove a general charitable intention). These are:

■ Where the relevant charity though no longer in being is deemed to exist in a different form at the date of the gift (for example, by having been amalgamated with other similar charities into a larger entity) as happened in *Re Faraker* [1912]. But, note *Re Stemson's WT* [1970], which signifies that the dissolution of an *incorporated charity* and transfer of its assets to another body will not be treated as existence in a different form.

■ Where the gift is construed not as a gift to the defunct charity as such but as a gift for its purposes and such purposes are capable of being fulfilled by other means.

The following points should be noted in this connection:

(a) The courts are most inclined to adopt this construction where there is a testamentary gift to an *unincorporated charity* by name with nothing more, and the charity has ceased to exist at the testator's death. See *Re Vernon's WT* [1972] and *Re Finger's WT* [1972].

(b) Where the gift is to an *incorporated charity* which has ceased to exist at the testator's death, it emerges from *Re Finger* that it will not ordinarily be construed as a gift for its purposes. It will accordingly fail unless the court can discern a general charitable intention which will enable it to invoke the *cy-pres* doctrine.

(c) Where the gift is to an incorporated charity which the court had ordered to be wound up but which had not yet been dissolved at the testator's death, the gift will not fail so as to invoke the *cy-pres* doctrine. Rather it will be treated as part of the charity's assets available on its eventual dissolution for distribution among its creditors. See *Re ARMS Ltd* [1997].

Gifts to charities which have never existed

Where a gift is made to a charity which has never existed at all, this will result in initial failure. It follows that the *cy-pres* doctrine will apply only if the donor had a general charitable intent. However, it appears from *Re Harwood* [1936] that the courts are more inclined to ascribe a general charitable intention to the donor in the case of a gift to a charity which never existed than in the case of one which once existed but became defunct.

Combined gifts to charitable and non-charitable bodies

A donor may direct that certain property should be divided among several named bodies. Where it happens that all these bodies are charities, except for one, the gift to the non-charitable body almost invariably fails, as happened in *Re Satterthwaite's WT* [1966] and *Re Jenkins' WT* [1966]; *Chichester Diocesan Fund v Simpson* [1944]; *AG Cayman Island v Even Wahr-Hansen* [2001].

An issue which arises in such cases is whether the fact that the gifts are predominantly in favour of charities is indicative of a general charitable intention on the donor's part. Judicial opinion is divided on the matter. Such an intention was held to exist in *Satterthwaite* and the court accordingly directed that the gift to the non-charitable body should be applied *cy-pres* towards charitable purposes.

By contrast, in *Jenkins*, the court refused to infer such an intention from the fact that all but one of the intended donees was charitable and concluded that there was no basis for applying the *cy-pres* doctrine to the share of the non-charitable body.

Subsequent failure

The *cy-pres* doctrine also comes into play in the event of the failure of a charitable gift after it has actually taken effect. Such subsequent failure may occur, for instance:

▨ where property is given to a charity which was in existence when the gift was made but which has since ceased to exist;

▨ where a gift is made to trustees for a charitable purpose which is carried on for some time but is then discontinued because it has become impossible or impracticable to sustain or is no longer considered suitable;

▨ where a gift is made to trustees for a charitable purpose which is duly completed leaving a surplus (as happened in *Re King*).

In the event of subsequent failure, because the property affected is already in the charitable domain, the *cy-pres* doctrine applies without any need to prove that the donor had a general charitable intention. This was made abundantly clear in *Re Slevin* [1891] where T left a legacy for an orphanage. This orphanage existed at T's death but was shut before T's will was administered. The court held that the gift would be applied *cy-pres* without regard to T's charitable intent since this was a case of subsequent failure, in that the orphanage was still in existence at the time of the gift. See also *Re Wright* [1954] and *Re Moon* [1948].

WIDENING OF THE *CY-PRES* DOCTRINE BY STATUTE

The Charities Act 1960 now re-enacted in the Charities Act 1993 (as amended by the Charities Act 2006) extended the *cy-pres* doctrine so that it is not confined to trusts which are impossible or impracticable to implement.

Occasions for applying property *cy-pres* under s 13 Charities Act 1993

It is provided in s 13 of the Charities Act 1993 that the original purposes of a charitable gift can be altered to allow the property or part of it to be applied *cy-pres* in the following circumstances:

■ where the original purpose has as far as possible been fulfilled;

■ where the original purpose cannot be carried out at all or carried out as directed or according to the spirit of the gift;

■ where the original purpose utilises only part of the property;

■ where the property and other property applicable for similar purposes can be more effectively pooled together and suitably applied towards common purposes;

■ where the gift was made by reference to a geographical area which has since ceased to be a unit or to a class of persons or area which has since ceased to be suitable or practicable; see *Peggs v Lamb* [1993];

■ where the original purpose has, since it was laid down:

  ● been adequately provided for by other means; or
  ● ceased, as being useless or harmful to the community or for other reasons, to be in law charitable; or
  ● ceased in any other way to provide a suitable and effective method of using the property .

See *Re Lepton's Charity* [1972] and *Varsani v Jesani* [1998].

In accordance with an amendment made by the Charities Act 2006, regard should also be had to the social and economic circumstances prevailing at the time of the proposed alteration of the original purposes.

Application of *cy-pres* to gifts of donors who are unknown or disclaiming

Where funds have been raised from the public for a charitable purpose which fails, s 14 of the Charities Act 1993 provides that:

- any contributor who either executes a disclaimer or does not come forward to reclaim his contribution after prescribed advertisements and inquiries have been made loses his entitlement and his contribution will be applied *cy-pres*;

- if funds have been raised in a manner not adapted for distinguishing one contribution from another (for example, collection boxes) or represent the proceeds of lotteries or similar activities, no advertisements or inquiries are required before such funds can be applied *cy-pres*.

You should now be confident that you would be able to tick all of the boxes on the checklist at the beginning of this chapter. To check your knowledge of Charitable trusts why not visit the companion website and take the Multiple Choice Question test. Check your understanding of the terms and vocabulary used in this chapter with the flashcard glossary.

Non-charitable purpose trusts, trusts of imperfect obligation and unincorporated associations

9

NON-CHARITABLE PURPOSE TRUSTS

The beneficiary principle – The general rule is that a non-charitable purpose trust, eg a trust created with the object of advancing the preservation of the independence and integrity of newspapers – *Re Astor's Settlement Trusts* [1952] is void. The main objection to such a trust is that there is no beneficiary to enforce it. A private trust has ascertainable beneficiaries to enforce the trust and although a charitable purpose trust does not have ascertainable beneficiaries, it will be enforced by the Attorney-General. In *Morice v Bishop of Durham* [1804], Grant MR held that 'there can be no trust, over the exercise of which, this court will not assume a control, for an uncontrollable power of disposition would be ownership and not trust ... There must be somebody in whose favour the court can decree performance.'

However, there are three purpose trusts which have been allowed despite the lack of a beneficiary. These exceptions have been stated by Roxburgh J in *Re Astor* 'as concessions to human weakness and sentiment and should not be extended'. They are called Trusts of Imperfect Obligation or Unenforceable Trusts.

Trusts of Imperfect Obligation

In these three exceptional cases, namely trusts for the erection or maintenance of monuments, tombs and graves; trusts for the care of specific animals and trusts for the saying of private masses, the trustee may be required to give the court an undertaking that the purpose will be carried out. Further, the trust will only be recognised if its purpose is *certain* – compare *Re Endacott* [1960] in which a bequest 'to the North Tawton Devon Parish Council for the purpose of providing some useful memorial to myself' failed because there were insufficient guidelines for it to be regarded as certain. Secondly, the trust *must not offend the rule against perpetuities* – in this context, the trust must not exceed a period of 21 years, and thirdly, the trust *must not be against public policy* being of no benefit and wasteful – thus in *Brown v Burdett* [1882] the court held that the testator's direction to seal up a house for 20 years was contrary to public policy as it served no useful purpose.

■ Trusts for the erection or maintenance of monuments, tombs and graves – see *Mussett v Bingle* [1876] and *Re Hooper* [1932]. In the latter case, a testator bequeathed property to trustees to provide for the care and upkeep of certain graves 'so far as they legally can do so', ie for 21 years.

▨ Trusts for the care of specific animals – whilst a trust or gift for the care of animals generally will be upheld as charitable, this does not apply to trusts for particular animals, eg the testator's pets, which are recognised as trusts of imperfect obligation – *Re Dean* [1889], *Pettingall v Pettingall* [1842]. Both these cases concerned the care of horses after the testator's death. Although horses can live longer than 21 years (the perpetuity period for purpose trusts), the issue was not addressed by the court.

▨ Trusts for the saying of a private mass – a trust fund set aside for the saying of a Catholic mass in public will be regarded as charitable – *Re Hetherington* [1989]. This would not be the case for a trust for the saying of a mass, eg for the soul of the deceased testator, if this were conducted privately. However, such a trust has been regarded as a trust of imperfect obligation by the House of Lords in *Bourne v Keane* [1919].

THE RULE IN *RE DENLEY*

Re Denley's Trust Deed [1969] concerned the transfer of land to trustees to be maintained and used as a sports field for the benefit of employees of a company. The issue concerned whether this was a purpose trust in which case it would be void, or whether it could be regarded as a valid private trust for the benefit of ascertainable beneficiaries. Goff J favoured the second interpretation and stated 'where then the trust, though expressed as a purpose, is directly or indirectly for the benefit of an individual or individuals, it seems to me that it is in general outside the mischief of the beneficiary principle.' However, compare the strict approach applied in *Re Grant's Will Trusts* [1979] and *Leahy v AG for New South Wales* [1959] below.

THE RULE AGAINST PERPETUITIES

This rule is covered at length in Land Law. Briefly, the rule has two branches –

▨ the rule against remoteness of vesting;

▨ the rule against inalienability.

Both rules are aimed at attempts by a settlor to tie up property (whether real or personal) for an indefinite period of time. To allow property to be rendered non-transferable or unmarketable either indefinitely or perpetually would be both socially and commercially undesirable. The subject was governed by the common law and the Perpetuities & Accumulations Act 1964.

Trust instruments created prior to 5th April 2010 continue to be governed by the common law and the Perpetuities & Accumulations Act 1964 but trust instruments rated after 5th April 2010 are governed by the Perpetuities & Accumulations Act 2009.

▓ **The rule against remoteness of vesting** – this is concerned with future interests and requires that the interests of beneficiaries must vest within the perpetuity period. There are different perpetuity periods, 21 years, a life in being plus 21 years, and a statutory perpetuity period of 80 years. Under s 3 of the Act, there is a 'wait and see' procedure, ie the trust will be void only if it does not vest within the perpetuity period (compare the common law, under which it would be void from the start if there was a possibility that it might vest outside the perpetuity period).

The Perpetuities & Accumulations Act 2009 preserves the 'wait and see' procedure in s 7 but s 5 provides a single perpetuity period of 125 years, which replaces the previous range of perpetuity periods.

▓ **The rule against inalienability** – this relates to purpose trusts and is concerned with the duration of such a trust. The rule does not apply to charitable purpose trusts but does apply to trusts of imperfect obligation, which are permitted to last for a perpetuity period of 21 years. The Perpetuities & Accumulations Act 2009 does not affect the rule against inalienability which applies to private purpose trusts.

The rule against excessive accumulations

Section 13 of the Perpetuities & Accumulations Act 2009 abolishes the rule against excessive accumulations of income (formerly governed by ss 164-166 of the Law of Property Act 1925 and s 13 of the Perpetuities & Accumulations Act 1964. This rule was created as a result of *Thelluson v Woodford* [1779] involving Peter Thelluson who in his will directed that the income from his estate should be accumulated (ie added to capital) rather than distributed to any of his descendants alive at the date of his death. The abolition of this rule means that subject to the rule against remoteness of vesting, which limits the life of a trust, trustees now have the power to accumulate income generated within settlements without restriction.

DEFINITION OF AN UNINCORPORATED ASSOCIATION (HEREAFTER REFERRED TO AS UA)

UA arises where a group of people (two or more) join together and pool property for a certain common purpose – eg to promote a political cause or to set up a sports club.

The group will usually have a set of rules (sometimes informal) concerning how it is to function and it will usually require property to help achieve its ends.

Lawton LJ in *Conservative and Unionist Central Office v Burrell* [1982] defined an 'unincorporated association' as:

- two or more persons
- bound together for one or more common purposes, not being business purposes,
- by mutual undertakings, each having mutual duties and obligations,
- in an organisation which has rules in respect of control of it and its funds; and
- which can be joined or left at will.

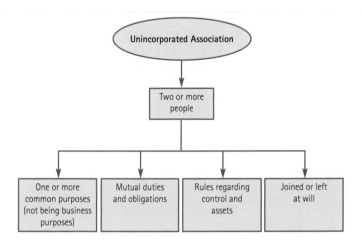

Not clear whether all the features need to be present – not essential that the association can be joined or left at will; also no obvious reason to exclude associations with business purposes.

Three key issues in UA:

1 how they acquire property

2 how property is held once acquired

3 what happens to property if the association comes to an end.

1. HOW THEY ACQUIRE PROPERTY

In principle, because it has no legal personality, gifts and donations cannot be made to unincorporated associations, nor can they be beneficiaries under a trust, nor act as trustees in their own right. However, bequests are often made to such associations, and frequently they benefit from testamentary gifts that purport to recognise them as valid trustees. Therefore the legal foundation for property-holding by unincorporated associations becomes an issue of paramount importance.

How does one transfer property to an unincorporated association? In *Leahy v AG for New South Wales* [1959] there were three possibilities:

(i) The donor could transfer the property to the existing members of the association beneficially.

Problems:
   (a) Members would be free to deal with the property as they see fit – they could simply take their share of the assets and leave. This would defeat the intentions of the donor, who has given the property for the association's purposes.
   (b) It doesn't provide for the fact of fluctuating membership of the group – the property becomes beneficially owned by the people who were members at the time of the transfer, not taking into account their current membership status or the interests of any new members who may have joined.

(ii) The donor could transfer the property beneficially to existing and future members of the association.

Problem:

A beneficial transfer to existing and future members provides for the group's fluctuating membership but would seem to tie the property up in perpetuity.

(iii) The donor could transfer the property on trust for the purposes of the association.

Problem:

Applying property for the purposes of the association may ensure utilisation in line with the donor's wishes but would fall foul of the beneficiary principle.

Options (ii) and (iii) above are not feasible, leaving only method (i). However, this would allow the members to ignore the donor's intentions and use the property with total freedom.

A method was sought to combat this and it was decided in *Re Recher's Will Trusts* [1972] that the best approach would be to consider any donation or legacy made to a UA as gifts 'to the members beneficially, not as joint tenants or as tenants in common so as to entitle each member to an immediate distributive share, but as an accretion to the funds which are the subject matter of the contract which the members have made inter se'. This became known as the contract holding theory. See also *Neville Estates v Madden* [1962].

The transfer to the members beneficially avoids the beneficiary principle problem but the real beauty of this theory as a solution is that the members have agreed to receive it as the group's property, as an accretion to the association's funds, and have bound themselves to utilise it in terms of the contract between themselves. Hence they do not have the right to sever a share and keep it for themselves.

In practice it is the treasurer who receives the property on trust for the group and ensures that it is utilised in line with the association's purposes, subject to the contract between the members. This also solves the problem of fluctuating membership. See also *Re Horley Town Football Club* [2006].

Example:

A wants to donate money to the Bux Mooting Society. If A simply transfers money 'to the Bux Mooting Society', it is clear that the group of members is to take the property beneficially. A could also leave the money 'on trust for the Bux Mooting Society' with the terms of transfer showing that the beneficial interest is once again to go to the group of members, even though the disposition is now termed a trust rather than an outright transfer. Both of these transfers would be acceptable under a *Re Recher* analysis.

Problem:

If A transfers money 'to the Bux Mooting Society' for a particular purpose (example: 'for encouraging debate' or 'for funding a negotiating competition'), A is seeking to dictate how the association is to use that money and it is clearly NOT going to the members beneficially. Because this creates a purpose trust it would fail unless it could be brought within one of the exceptions to the beneficiary principle.

Solution:

Discounting any reference to the purposes – this allows us to treat the donation as a gift to the members beneficially. We can do this by arguing that the purposes were merely suggestions as to how the money might be used or they simply reflected the general motives of the donor *Re Osoba* [1979] when making the donation, without imposing a strict obligation to carry it out. (*Re Lipinski's Will Trusts* [1976].)

▌ In Re LIPINSKI'S WILL TRUSTS [1976]

Basic facts

L bequeathed half of his estate to an association which was non-charitable and unincorporated, 'to be used solely in the work of constructing or improving buildings for the association'. His executors questioned the validity of the bequest.

The court held that the specified purpose was within the power of the association and its members for the time being were the ascertained or ascertainable beneficiaries. Accordingly, the gift was a valid gift.

Relevance

Where the purpose prescribed is clearly intended for the benefit of ascertained or ascertainable beneficiaries a gift with a superadded direction is valid.

The beneficiaries, the members of the association for the time being, are the persons who could enforce the purpose and they must, as it seems to me, be entitled not to enforce it or, indeed, to vary it.

The beneficiaries able to enforce the trust or, in the exercise of their contractual rights, to terminate the trust for their own benefit. Where the donee association is itself the beneficiary of the prescribed purpose, the gift should be construed as an absolute one subject to the contract.

▶ Re GRANT'S WILL TRUSTS [1980]

Basic facts

The deceased left property to the Labour Party property committee. It was not a gift to the members of the UA as joint tenants, and therefore could be valid only as a gift to them beneficially, subject to their contractual rights and obligations as members; it was not such a gift since the members' power to deal with the property was subject to the ultimate control of the National Executive Committee.

Relevance

A gift to a non-charitable association, which does not create a trust, cannot be valid, except where it may be construed as a gift to the existing members of the association, either as joint tenants or beneficially, subject to their contractual rights and obligations as members.

2. HOW PROPERTY IS HELD ONCE ACQUIRED

Because UA's are unincorporated, they have no legal personality separate from their members and therefore cannot hold any property in their own right. To overcome this problem, any property to be held for the UA must be vested in one or more of its members.

Look at the rules of the UA to determine which of the members will 'own' the property:

1 All the members could be co-owners at law, having entered into an agreement some whereby each individual undertakes to ensure that group property is used exclusively for the purposes of the association.
2 One or more of the members (usually the treasurer) becomes owner of the property at law, holding it on trust for the members as a collective. In practice, this is far more common.

Therefore, at any given moment, the property will be owned by the members as a whole or by one or more members acting as trustees for the collective, having agreed to be restricted in their dealings with the property as laid out in the contract between themselves.

EXAM ISSUES

(i) When a new member joins, does he immediately enter into a contract with all the other members individually? Can this bind him to follow the association's rules? Look at the rules of contract formation.
(ii) What effect does fluctuating membership have on the ownership of the group property? We have said that the property is held on trust for the group. This means that each member has an equitable interest under that trust. For the sake of continuity of the UA and to ensure fulfilment of the donor's intentions, it is assumed that when members leave, they relinquish any interest they have in the property and that new members acquire such an interest upon joining. In practice membership changes are seldom accompanied by formal documentation but it appears nevertheless as if the members are either disposing of or gaining equitable interests. The courts have not examined this area but it is clear that to make an effective disposition of one's equitable interest under a trust it must be made in writing and signed (s 53(1)(c) of the Law of Property Act 1925). This does seem to be an area ripe for discussion and could be useful for the more advanced student.

3. WHAT HAPPENS TO PROPERTY IF THE ASSOCIATION COMES TO AN END

Initially, only two options:

(i) the property would revert back to those who provided it by way of a resulting trust, or
(ii) it would be deemed 'ownerless' and vest in the Crown (*bona vacantia*).

Re West Sussex Constabulary's Widows, Children and Benevolent Fund Trusts [1971].

What happens to any surplus depends on how the money was raised:

(i) contributions from members themselves

Treated as ownerless (*bona vacantia*) and became Crown property. Members' benefits were governed by the terms of their contract – they paid subscriptions so that in the event of their death money would be paid to their widows or dependents, who were third parties. They had no rights in the fund itself and couldn't share in any money left over should the fund be brought to an end.

(ii) raffles and sweepstakes

Also *bona vacantia* – those who paid did so under a contract (to take part in the raffle or sweepstake) and so, like the members, could have no rights beyond those conferred by that contract.

(iii) collecting boxes

Also *bona vacantia* – contributors must be regarded as having parted with the money 'out-and-out', with no intention of it being returned, even in the event of the fund's dissolution.

(iv) donations and legacies

Returned to donors by means of resulting trust – donors had intended that the money should be retained by the donees only so long as the fund was in existence, and so any unused balance should be returned to them (applying *Re the Trusts of the Abbott Fund*).

EXAM ISSUES

(i) What is the basis for the distinction between donations made via the collecting boxes and the other donations encompassing more substantial legacies?

(ii) Is buying raffle tickets or entering a sweepstake not simply a different form of donation?

(iii) How could the money be declared *bona vacantia*? For such a finding the Court would have to have found that the fund was ownerless. As it was not ownerless before the fund was wound up, how did it suddenly become ownerless when the members decide to bring the fund to an end?

(iv) How can there be a resulting trust? This only makes sense if we say that the money was until then held on a purpose trust and this would contravene the beneficiary principle.

The contract holding theory was accepted as a solution to this problem in *Re Bucks Constabulary Widows' and Orphans' Fund Friendly Society (No 2)* [1979] – the members at the time of dissolution are each entitled to an equal share in the association's property because they are equally beneficially entitled to that property.

While an unincorporated association is in existence, the property is beneficially owned by the members but their use of their property is restricted by the terms of their contract. If the members decide to terminate the UA they are removing any restrictions placed by that contract on their use of the property and, as beneficial owners, are now free to deal with the property as they wish.

The members are free to agree to some other basis of distribution of the group's property upon dissolution, even where there is no express term to that effect *Re Sick and Funeral Society of St John's Sunday School* [1973].

Past members have no rights in the group's assets, only those members at the time of dissolution can claim any share of the property – *Re Bucks Constabulary*.

It therefore becomes acutely important to know exactly when the association was dissolved. Easy where the dissolution is by a vote of the members or a court order. But see *Re William Denby & Sons Ltd Sick and Benevolent Fund* [1971] and *Re St Andrew's Allotment Association* [1969].

There is an exception to the rule that the group's property is to be distributed among the members upon its dissolution. This is where, by death or resignation, the society is reduced to one member – in such a case the property is be regarded as ownerless, and so goes to the Crown as *bona vacantia*. See *Re Bucks Constabulary*.

See also *Davis v Richards and Wallington Industries* [1990].

However, in *Hanchett-Stamford v Attorney General* [2008] on the death of Mrs Hanchett Stamford, the sole surviving member of a non-charitable unincorporated association (the Performing & Capital Animals Defence League), the Court had to decide whether the surplus assets of the League formed part of her estate and could therefore pass in accordance with her wishes to the Born Free Foundation, or whether they passed to the Crown as *bona vacantia* in accordance with the *obiter dicta* of Walton J in *Re Bucks*. Lewison J said that the principle of vesting ownership in a sole surviving member was akin to the vesting of ownership in a sole surviving joint tenant where the rule of survivorship applied, and that it would be contrary to human rights law which prevents the deprivation of property except in the public interest.

You should now be confident that you would be able to tick all of the boxes on the checklist at the beginning of this chapter. To check your knowledge of Non–charitable purpose trusts, trusts of imperfect obligation and unincorporated associations why not visit the companion website and take the Multiple Choice Question test. Check your understanding of the terms and vocabulary used in this chapter with the flashcard glossary.

10

Trustees and administration of the trusts

How is an initial trustee appointed?

How are subsequent trustees appointed?

When may a trustee retire?

How is a trustee removed?

When may a trustee be remunerated?

What is meant by a trustee's fiduciary duty?

What principles must be taken into account when a trustee makes investments?

What is meant by a power of maintenance?

When may the statutory power of maintenance be exercised?

When does an interest carry the intermediate income?

What is meant by a power of advancement?

When may a statutory power of advancement be exercised?

Describe the statutory power of delegation by a trustee

Variation of trusts

When may the court vary a trust under its inherent jurisdiction?

When may the court sanction a variation under the Variation Act 1958?

What is meant by 'benefit' in this context?

What weight is given to the settlor's intention?

APPOINTMENT, RETIREMENT AND REMOVAL OF TRUSTEES

APPOINTMENT OF TRUSTEES

Capacity

As a general rule, any human being or corporate body with the capacity to own property may be appointed a trustee.

The appointment of infants as trustees is specifically prohibited by s 20 of the Law of Property Act (LPA) 1925 (though infants have been held to be trustees under resulting trusts in *Re Vinogradoff* [1935] and *Re Muller* [1953]).

Number of trustees

It is open to a settlor to specify a minimum or maximum number of trustees in the trust instrument. Where a minimum of two trustees is prescribed, a trust corporation may administer the trust as sole trustee. See *Re Duxbury's ST* [1993].

Where the trust instrument is silent, there is no upper or lower limit on the number of trustees a settlor/testator may appoint. However, it is inadvisable to appoint only one or to appoint too many.

Where the trust relates to real property, there is no strict lower limit but at least two trustees are usually appointed since a sole trustee of land cannot give a valid receipt to a purchaser if it is sold. An upper limit of four is imposed by s 34(2) of the Trustee Act (TA) 1925, but this limit is dispensed with where the land is held on trust for charitable, ecclesiastical or public purposes.

Procedure for appointing trustees

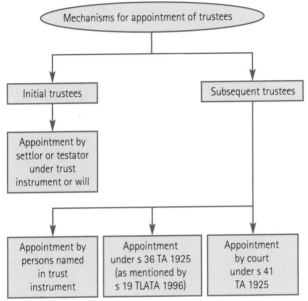

Appointment of the initial trustees

In the case of *inter vivos* trusts, the trustees are usually named in the trust instrument by the settlor (who may himself be one of the trustees); while in the case of testamentary trusts, the trustees are usually named by the testator in his will.

It sometimes happens that there are no initial trustees available to administer a trust at its inception. In such an event, the operative principle is expressed in the equitable maxim that 'a trust will not fail for want of trustees'.

In line with this principle, the courts have been prepared to give effect to testamentary trusts where no trustee was named in the will or all the trustees so named died before the testator or disclaimed the trust. See, for example, *Re Smirthwaite* [1871] and *Dodkin v Brunt* [1868].

By the same token, it has been held that, where a settlor has executed an *inter vivos* transfer or conveyance to trustees then living, the trust will not fail if the trustees all later die or disclaim the property. See, for example, *Jones v Jones* [1874] and *Mallott v Wilson* [1903].

Appointment of subsequent trustees

The need may arise from time to time to appoint new trustees *in place of* or *in addition to* the initial trustees. This can be done by inserting an express power of appointment in the trust instrument in favour of the settlor or in favour of some other person.

Section 36 of the TA 1925: Considerable scope also exists for the appointment of replacement and additional trustees under s 36 of the TA 1925.

Replacement trustees: Under s 36(1) and (2), one or more new trustees may be appointed in place of a trustee who:

- is dead;

- remains outside the UK for a continuous period of 12 months;

- desires to be discharged from the trust or refuses to act or is unfit to act (for example, due to bankruptcy or criminal dishonesty);

- is incapable of acting (for example, due to old age or mental disorder) or is an infant; or

- has been removed from the trust in the exercise of a power contained in the trust instrument.

The power of appointing replacement trustees lies with:

- any person nominated in the trust instrument for this purpose;

- the surviving or continuing trustee(s) for the time being; or

- the personal representatives of the last surviving/continuing trustee (in that order).

Additional trustees: Limited scope for appointing additional trustees exists under s 36(1) since it allows for a departing trustee to be replaced by one or more trustees.

For the most part, additional trustees are appointed under s 36(6). Appointments can be made under s 36(6) even if no trustee is being replaced, provided there are no more than three trustees administering the trust and the number after appointment will not exceed four. Under s 36(6), such appointments are to be made by the person(s) nominated for this purpose by the trust instrument or, if there is no such person, by the trustee(s) for the time being.

Section 36(6) has been amended by the Trustee Delegation Act 1999. This Act enlarges the categories of persons who may appoint additional trustees to include a donee of a power of attorney granted by all the trustees who intends to exercise trust functions relating to land.

Section 41 of the TA 1925 empowers the court to appoint trustees in addition to or in place of existing trustees where it is expedient to make an appointment but it is found to be inexpedient, difficult or impracticable to do so under the trust instrument or under s 36.

Examples of situations in which the courts will intervene are:

- where the parties entitled to appoint new trustees are not in a position to do so for reasons such as:

    - infancy: *Re Parsons* [1940]
    - old age/infirmity: *Re Phelps ST* [1886]
    - wartime disruptions: *Re May's WT* [1941];

- where the last surviving trustee dies intestate and there is no one to administer his estate;

- where all the trustees named in a will pre-decease the testator: see *Re Smirthwaite* [1871];

- where an appointment is delayed unduly because of disagreements between those empowered to appoint new trustees: see *Re Tempest* [1866].

Re Tempest is also notable because it identified the factors that the court would consider in exercising its jurisdiction, namely:

- the wishes of the settlor and the beneficiaries;

- whether the appointee is likely to favour some beneficiaries at the expense of others; and

■ whether the appointment is likely to promote or impede the execution of the trust.

Section 19 of TLATA 1996 provides that where:

■ there is no person expressly nominated by the trust instrument for the purpose of appointing new trustees; and

■ the beneficiaries are all of full age and capacity and absolutely entitled to the trust property,

these beneficiaries may give written directions to the trustee(s) for the time being to appoint the person(s) specified in such directions as new trustees of the trust.

Accepting or disclaiming the trust: A trustee may signify his acceptance of the trust by deed, by ordinary writing or orally. In addition, acceptance may be implied where, for example:

■ a person named as an executor/trustee in a will obtains probate of the will: see *Mucklow v Fuller* [1821] and *Re Sharman's WT* [1942]; or

■ a person named as a trustee interferes with the trust property in some way: see *James v Frearson* [1842] and *Urch v Walker* [1838].

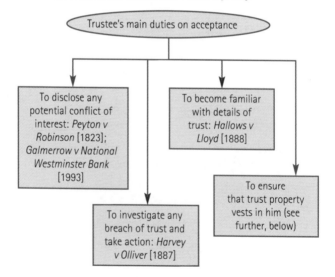

A trustee may disclaim the trust by turning down his appointment before acceptance. Such a disclaimer may be by deed, in writing or oral; or it may be inferred from the trustee's conduct (for example, where he neglects to assume office, as in *Clout v Frewer* [1924]).

Procedure for vesting:

- In the case of an initial trustee, trust property vests in him, where he is named in the trust deed.

- With regard to a subsequent trustee, s 40(1) of the TA 1925 provides that once he has been appointed by deed, this automatically vests the property in the new trustee jointly with the existing ones.

- There are, however, certain types of property which do not vest automatically where a new trustee is appointed by deed, notably:

  - land mortgaged as security for money owed to the trust;

  - land held under a lease, which contains a covenant not to assign without consent;

  - stocks and shares.

RETIREMENT OF TRUSTEES

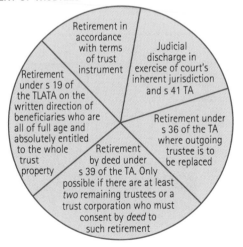

Retirement in accordance with terms of trust instrument

Judicial discharge in exercise of court's inherent jurisdiction and s 41 TA

Retirement under s 19 of the TLATA on the written direction of beneficiaries who are all of full age and absolutely entitled to the whole trust property

Retirement under s 36 of the TA where outgoing trustee is to be replaced

Retirement by deed under s 39 of the TA. Only possible if there are at least *two* remaining trustees or a trust corporation who must consent by *deed* to such retirement

A trustee may retire from a trust in five ways.

1 Under an express power given in the trust instrument – this is rare.

2 Under s 36 Trustee Act 1925 (see under 'Appointment') where the retiring trustee is replaced by a new trustee.

3 Under s 39 Trustee Act 1925. This allows a trustee to retire (by deed) without being replaced provided at least two trustees or a trust corporation remain after his retirement.

4 Under s 41 Trustee Act 1925 (see under 'Appointment') which gives the court power to discharge a trustee when it replaces him with a new trustee.

5 Under s 19 Trusts of Land and Appointment of Trustees Act 1996 (see earlier) where the beneficiaries if *sui juris* and together absolutely entitled direct a trustee to retire. The trustee must declare his retirement by deed and, unless he is to be replaced, at least two trustees or a trust corporation must remain after his retirement.

REMOVAL OF TRUSTEES

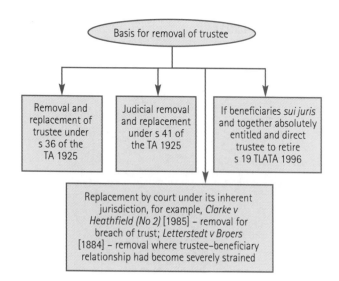

Under s 41 Trustee Act 1925, the court may remove a trustee on the appointment of a new trustee (see under 'Appointment'). The court also has inherent jurisdiction to remove a trustee compulsorily – see *Letterstedt v Broers* [1884] in which it was stated by Lord Blackburn: 'In exercising so delicate a jurisdiction as that of removing trustees, their Lordships do not venture to lay down any general rule beyond the very broad principle that their main guide must be the welfare of the beneficiaries.'

Under s 19 TLATA (see under 'Retirement'), the beneficiaries may direct a trustee to retire.

THE MAIN DUTIES AND POWERS OF TRUSTEES

THE NATURE OF THE TRUSTEE'S RESPONSIBILITIES

The position of the trustee carries such heavy responsibilities that it is 'an act of great kindness in anyone to accept it' – *per* Lord Hardwicke in *Knight v Earl of Plymouth* [1747].

A trustee's basic functions are to perform duties and exercise the powers provided for in the trust instrument as well as general duties and powers prescribed by statute or by the courts.

Duties are obligatory. Accordingly, a beneficiary may proceed against the trustee for breach of trust if he fails to perform a duty. By contrast, the trustee's powers are discretionary, although they are held in a fiduciary capacity and so the trustee must consider periodically whether to exercise them or not. The beneficiary cannot dictate the manner in which the trustee is to exercise his powers: see *Re Beloved Wilkes Charity* [1851]; *Re Londonderry's ST* [1965]; and *Wilson and Another v The Law Debenture Trust Corp* [1995]. Furthermore, the courts will not ordinarily interfere to circumscribe the exercise of a trustee's discretions unless he has acted dishonestly, capriciously, erroneously or without proper judgment: see *Re Manisty's Settlement* [1974] and *Turner v Turner* [1984].

Note, however, that s 11 of TLATA 1996 contemplates that in the exercise of their powers, trustees of *land* shall:

- so far as practicable consult any beneficiaries who are of full age and beneficially entitled to an interest in possession; and

- so far as consistent with the general interest of the trust, give effect to the wishes of those beneficiaries.

Note, also, the power to appoint and dismiss trustees collectively exercisable under s 19 of the TLATA 1996 by beneficiaries who are of full age and absolutely entitled to trust property; this now enables such beneficiaries to assert much greater control over the exercise of trustees' powers than had hitherto been the case.

THE UNANIMITY RULE

Where there are several trustees, each one is required to participate fully in administering the trust. This requirement means that trustees must exercise their powers unanimously unless there is a provision to the contrary in the trust instrument: see *Luke v South Kensington Hotel* [1879]; *Re Mayo* [1943]; and *Re Butlin's ST* [1976]. But, note that the rule does not apply to charitable trusts: see *Perry v Shipway* [1859] and *Re Whitely* [1910]. In respect of charitable trusts the trustees may execute transactions by reference to majority decisions.

REMUNERATION OF TRUSTEE

Historically, the office of trustee was a gratuitous one, that is, the trustee was not entitled to payment for administering the trust (*Robinson v Pett* [1734]). The administration of modern trusts is a complex and time consuming business and charging for services became more common by various means:

■ inserting a charging clause into the trust instrument;

■ through the inherent jurisdiction of the court (*Re Duke of Norfolk's ST* [1981]; *Foster v Spencer* [1995]);

■ where the beneficiaries who are *sui juris* agree to pay the trustee;

■ where the trustee is a solicitor and the rule in *Cradock v Piper* [1850] applies;

■ where the trust includes assets in a foreign country and persons administering such assets are entitled to payment under the laws of that country;

■ where payment is authorised by statute.

The Trustee Act 2000 reversed the presumption that trustees should not be paid and, except where the trust instrument prohibits payment, the trustee is entitled to be remunerated for any service to the trust, even if that service could have been performed by a lay trustee.

The remuneration code is set out in ss 28–33, dealing with remuneration and payment of expenses to trustees, and also remuneration and payment of expenses to agents, nominees and custodians.

The remuneration code applies to services provided or expenses incurred after the coming into force of the Act (February 2001).

THE STANDARD OF CARE

The trustee must exercise a high degree of diligence in carrying out the trust. In particular:

- an *unpaid trustee* (for example, the settlor's friend/relation) must in executing the trust take 'all those precautions which an ordinary prudent man of business would take in managing similar affairs of his own', *per* Lord Blackburn in *Speight v Gaunt* [1883];

- cases such as *Re Waterman's WT* [1952] and *Bartlett v Barclays Bank Trust Co* [1980] as well as the Law Reform Committee's Report on the *Powers and Duties of Trustees* (1982) signify that a paid trustee is subject to a 'higher standard of diligence and knowledge' or a 'special duty to display expertise' as compared to an unpaid trustee. They do not, however, shed further light on the precise standard demanded of paid trustees.

EXAM ISSUE: The duty of care is now on a statutory basis, as set out in s 1 of the Trustee Act 2000. A trustee must exercise such care and skill as is reasonable in the circumstances, and in particular:

(a) to any special knowledge or expertise that he holds himself out as having; and

(b) if he acts as a trustee in the course of business or a profession, to any special knowledge or expertise that it is reasonable to expect of a person acting in the course of that kind of business or profession.

THE TRUSTEE'S DUTIES

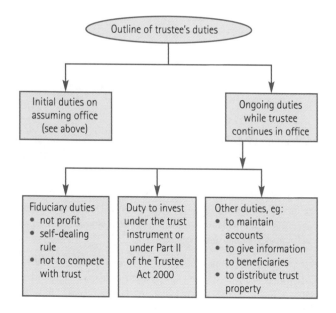

FIDUCIARY DUTIES

These are duties imposed by equity with a view to ensuring that a trustee's interests do not conflict with those of the trust.

(a) EXAM ISSUES: Unauthorised profits

As stated in Chapter 6, when dealing with constructive trusts, a trustee or other fiduciary 'is not, unless otherwise expressly provided, entitled to make a profit', *per* Lord Herschell in *Bray v Ford* [1896].

Cases discussed in that chapter, like *Sugden v Crossland* [1876]; *Williams v Barton* [1927]; *Re Macadam* [1945]; *Keech v Sandford* [1726]; *Regal (Hastings) v Gulliver* [1942]; and *Boardman v Phipps* [1967], establish that a trustee or other fiduciary will be required to hold such profits on constructive trust for their principal.

▶ Re MACADAM [1945]

Basic facts

Trustees under a will had been appointed directors of a company and applied to court to determine whether they were liable to account to the estate for remuneration received in the form of director's fees.

Held, that, although the remuneration was for services as directors of the company, the opportunity to obtain that remuneration was gained as a result of a discretion vested in the trustees, and that they were liable to account to the trust estate for the sums received by them as remuneration for those services.

Relevance

Trustees were held liable to account for directors' fees where trust shareholding was used to vote themselves into office. As a rule of thumb, to avoid any semblance of impropriety, trustees should use any shareholding they control to vote AGAINST themselves.

▶ BOARDMAN v PHIPPS [1967]

Basic facts

Trustees, in their personal capacity, acquired a controlling holding in a company in order to manage it more profitably and increase the value of its shares, which formed a large part of the trust's assets. The trust did not initially have the necessary capital to acquire the shares.

The court said they had placed themselves in a special position, which was of a fiduciary character, in relation to the negotiations relating to the trust shares and that out of such special position they obtained the opportunity to make a profit out of the shares and knowledge that the profit was there to be made. A profit was made and they were accountable accordingly.

However, the court held that that they had acted openly, in a manner which was highly beneficial to the trust and accordingly were entitled in the circumstances to payment on a liberal scale for their work and skill.

Relevance

It is an inflexible rule of a Court of Equity that a person in a fiduciary position is not, unless otherwise expressly provided, entitled to make a profit; he is not allowed to put himself in a position where his interest and duty conflict (*Bray v Ford* [1896]).

The liability in no way depends on fraud, or absence of bona fides; or whether the plaintiff has in fact been damaged or benefited by his action. The liability arises from the mere fact of a profit having been made.

▶ REGAL (HASTINGS) v GULLIVER [1942]

Basic facts

Regal had considered applying for shares in a subsidiary company, but had been unable to afford them, whereupon the directors subscribed for shares on their own account and made a profit. The directors would not have been in a position to profit had they not been directors, but arguably there was no conflict of interest, given that Regal was not in a position to subscribe on its own account. The directors were nevertheless held liable to account.

Relevance

Fiduciaries liable to account for profits derived from fiduciary position *even* in good faith (eg investments actually coincidentally beneficial to company itself).

(b) Purchase of trust property by trustee

Trustees who decide to sell trust property 'have an overriding duty to obtain the best price which they can for their beneficiaries', *per* Wynn-Parry J in *Buttle v Saunders* [1950].

The self-dealing rule: If a trustee is able to purchase trust property he will be tempted not to seek the best possible price. In view of this, equity has evolved the self-dealing rule under which a sale of trust property to a trustee (as well as a sale of a trustee's property to the trust) is voidable by a beneficiary. Four points should be noted regarding the self-dealing rule:

1 a sale to a trustee may be set aside even if he bought in good faith and at a fair price: see *Ex p James* [1803]; *Ex p Lacey* [1802];

2 if the arrangement is that trust property will be sold to a trustee after he retires, the sale may also be set aside: see *Wright v Morgan* [1926], unless the sale takes place long after his retirement: see *Re Boles* [1902];

3 a sale of trust property may be set aside where a trustee is in effect indirectly buying it through another person (see *Delves v Gray* [1902]) or through a company in which he has a substantial shareholding (see *Re Thompson's Settlement* [1986]);

4 the courts will not set aside a sale on the basis of this rule:
   - where the purchaser is made a trustee after contracting to buy trust property but before completion: see *Re Mulholland's WT* [1949] and *Spiro v Glencrown Ltd* [1996];
   - where the purchaser is a bare trustee with no active duties to perform: see *Parkes v White* [1805];
   - where there are special circumstances which in the court's view make it inappropriate to set aside the sale: see *Clark v Clark* [1884] and *Holder v Holder* [1968].

The fair-dealing rule: the self-dealing rule does not apply where a trustee purchases a beneficiary's interest in trust property (as distinct from purchasing the trust property itself): see *Ex p Lacey* [1802].

The operative rule in such cases is the fair-dealing rule under which the beneficiary cannot set aside the sale once the trustee is able to show 'that he has taken no advantage of his position and made full disclosure to the beneficiary and that the transaction was fair and honest', *per* Megarry VC in *Tito v Waddell (No 2)* [1977]: see also *Coles v Trecothick* [1804]; *Thomas v Eastwood* [1877]; and *Dougan v MacPherson* [1902].

(c) Competing in business with the trust

A conflict may occur between the duties of a trustee and his personal interest where the trust estate includes a business and the trustee is found to be conducting a business of his own in competition with the trust. Such a conflict arose, for instance, in *Re Thompson* [1930] where the trust estate included a yacht broking business and an injunction was granted to restrain a trustee from embarking on this line of business in the same town.

THE DUTY TO INVEST

Historically trusts were concerned with family settlements. The primary duty of the trustees was to preserve the fund for future generations. Nowadays the administration of trusts is concerned primarily with investment and growth.

A well-drafted trust instrument often contains an express investment clause. Where the trust instrument is silent, the Trustee Act 2000 provides 'the general power of investment'. Section 3(1) provides: '... a trustee may make any kind of investment that he could make if he were absolutely entitled to the assets of the trust'.

The general power of investment has replaced the complex and much criticised provisions of the Trustee Investment Act (TIA) 1961, both prospectively and retrospectively.

The general power of investment can be excluded or restricted by the trust instrument (s 6).

General principles to be taken into account in making investments

(a) Trustees must exercise a higher degree of care than in performing other duties

This is implicit in the remarks of Lord Watson in *Learoyd v Whiteley* [1887] who declared that a trustee must when investing trust assets spurn any investment which is attended with hazard. His duty is not merely:

> ... to take such care only as a prudent man would take if he had only himself to consider. The duty rather is to take such care as an ordinary prudent man would take if he were minded to make an investment for other people for whom he felt morally obliged to provide.

At the same time, Bacon VC was quick to emphasise in *Re Godfrey* [1883] that no investment can ever be guaranteed to be completely safe since all human affairs carry some degree of risk. This stance is also evident in cases like *Re*

Chapman [1896] which held that a trustee who acts honestly and in good faith in making investment decisions, will not be liable for any ensuing loss, simply because the benefit of hindsight shows that he was wrong.

Furthermore, the traditional insistence that trustees should refrain from investments attended by hazard has been tempered by the increasing acceptance of the 'portfolio theory' in the realm of trust investments. In the words of Hoffman J in *Nestlé v National Westminster Bank* [1993], 'modern trustees acting within their investment powers are entitled to be judged by the standards of the current portfolio theory which emphasises the risk of the entire portfolio rather than the risk attaching to each investment taken in isolation'. This suggests in effect that an investment with a potentially high return which on its own may be considered unduly speculative may be justified if it is appropriately balanced by other safer investments within the same portfolio.

(b) Trustees must diversify their investments

It is desirable for trustees to diversify their investments so that even if some of them fail to yield dividend others will do so. Section 4 of the Trustee Act 2000 sets out standard investment criteria, including the requirement to review the investments from time to time (s 4(2)) and to consider the need for diversification, in so far as it is appropriate to the circumstances of the trust (s 4(2)(b)). However, in *Gregson v HAE Trustees Ltd* [2009], it was stated that trustees could decide against diversification of investments if the settlor had instructed that particular assets should be retained by the trust fund.

(c) Trustees must maintain a balance between income and capital

Trustees are bound to act fairly as between different classes of beneficiaries. They must thus select investments which as far as possible yield a reasonable income while preserving the capital value of the trust assets.

It is inappropriate, for example, for trustees to invest in:

- wasting assets which yield a high income while their capital value steadily depreciates (for example, short leases and copyrights); or

- objects which are likely to appreciate in value over time but which yield little or no income (for example, antiques and paintings).

(d) Trustees should not ordinarily be guided by non-financial considerations

Buttle v Saunders [1950] held that in selling trust property, a trustee must seek the best financial interests of the beneficiaries without regard to underlying ethical implications. In *Cowan v Scargill* [1985], the same stance was adopted in connection with the trustee's duty to invest.

The extent to which ethical considerations should feature in investment decisions poses particular problems in the case of charitable trustees. In the leading case of *Harries v The Church Commissioners* [1992], the court acknowledged that ethical considerations may be material to the extent that charitable trustees may opt not to invest in a highly profitable sector or venture if the investment:

■ conflicts directly with the charity's objects; or

■ is liable to alienate potential donors or beneficiaries.

The specific issue which fell to be determined in *Harries* was whether the Church Commissioners as trustees of Church of England assets were required to restrict their investments to those which sought to promote the Christian faith even if this meant not maximising the return on investments. The court held that charitable trustees, like other trustees, had a duty to maximise their profits and that their investments could only be dictated by ethical considerations to the extent that this did not detract from their duty. The fact that the Commissioners were pursuing an investment policy which excluded investments in armaments, tobacco, gambling, etc, was considered acceptable by the court since there was a sufficiently wide range of alternative investments open to them to ensure profitability.

The Trustee Act 2000 makes provision for investing in freehold or leasehold land (s 8). Section 6(3) and (4) of TLATA 1996 also makes provision for investment in land.

OTHER DUTIES OF THE TRUSTEE

(a) Duty to distribute

Trustees must distribute trust property according to the settlor's wishes. Depending on the circumstances, this may entail the payment of income or the transfer of the trust assets or part thereof to the rightful beneficiaries.

Trustees who make a distribution in favour of a person who is not the rightful beneficiary may be liable for breach of trust: see, for example, *Eaves v Hickson* [1861] and *Re Diplock* [1948].

The trustees may, however, safeguard themselves against liability for wrongful distribution:

- by preliminary inquiries and advertisements under s 27 of the TA 1925 for prospective beneficiaries to come forward: see *Re Aldhous* [1955];

- by obtaining *Benjamin orders* in cases where the entitlement of a beneficiary is not in doubt but it is uncertain whether he is still alive: see, for example, *Re Benjamin* [1902] and *Re Green's WT* [1985];

- by insuring against the possibility that a beneficiary whose continued existence or whereabouts is in doubt may subsequently emerge: see *Evans v Westcombe* [1999];

- by applying for appropriate directions in cases where the trustees are unable to resolve a particular issue concerning the distribution of the estate (for example, because the trust is ambiguous).

Where the intended beneficiaries cannot be traced or distribution proves to be impossible or impracticable for some other reason, trustees may as a last resort pay the trust fund into court, as happened in *Re Gillingham Bus DF* [1958].

(b) Duty to keep accounts and provide information
As seen from *Pearse v Green* [1819], a trustee must keep proper accounts.

Such accounts must be open to the beneficiaries who may also require general information from the trustees on the affairs of the trust. Discussions and decisions of trustees are often documented in trust diaries, minute books, etc and *O'Rourke v Darbishire* [1920] held that 'the beneficiary is entitled to see all [such] documents because they are ... in a sense his own'.

This right of access to trust documents was qualified by *Re Londonderry's ST* [1965] in relation to documents which record the reasons for the exercise of the trustee's discretions.

This decision has been affected by the Privy Council decision (not strictly binding) of *Schmidt v Rosewood Trust* [2003], which held that:

- no beneficiary has any entitlement as of right to trust documents;

- the right to seek disclosure was an aspect of the court's jurisdiction;

- the court had to carry out a balancing exercise weighing the interests of claimants, trustees and third parties.

THE TRUSTEE'S POWERS

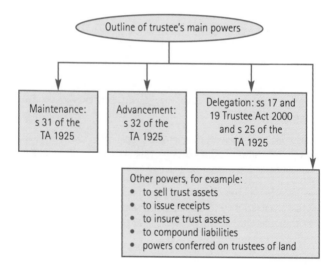

The power of maintenance

A trustee cannot obtain a valid receipt for any income paid to an infant beneficiary (IB). He must either retain the income or apply it towards the IB's maintenance, education or benefit under the terms of the trust instrument or by virtue of the power of maintenance in s 31 of the TA 1925. Any income not used to maintain the IB in a given year is accumulated with a view to being invested in authorised securities or carried over and applied towards his future maintenance.

In exercising this power, the trustee is enjoined by s 31 to have regard to:

> ... the age of the infant and his requirements and generally to the circumstances of his case and in particular to what other income is available for the same purpose.

Conditions for exercising the power of maintenance in s 31

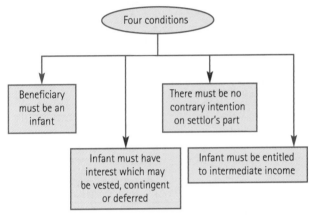

(a) The beneficiary must be an infant
Once an IB attains majority, any income accruing from the trust property or his share thereof becomes payable to him unless the trust instrument provides otherwise.

(b) The trust property from which the income is derived (or a part thereof) must be held on trust for the IB in whose favour the power is exercised

(c) The trustee must not be deprived of the power of maintenance by a contrary intention in the trust instrument
For example:

■ a direction to pay the income to someone other than IB; or

■ a direction to accumulate the income.

See *Re Ransome* [1957]; *IRC v Bernstein* [1961]; and *Re McGeorge* [1963].

(d) The nature of the IB's interest must be such that he is entitled to the intermediate income accruing during infancy
The position in this regard may be summarised in the chart overleaf.

Payment of income to IB's parents for his maintenance: Instead of applying income generated by the trust property in maintaining an IB, the trustees may

Nature of interest	Does it carry the intermediate income?
1 Vested interest	Yes: unless settlor intends otherwise
2 Contingent interest under *vivos inter* trust	Yes: unless settlor intends otherwise
3. Contingent interest under testamentary trust: (i) specific bequest/devise (ii) residuary bequest/devise (iii) pecuniary legacy	Yes Yes Only in the following events: ■ testator is parent or *parentis in loco* to IB and will makes no other provision for IB; ■ will reveals intention that legacy is to be used to maintain IB; ■ will directs that legacy is to be set apart from testator's estate
4. Deferred/future interest under testamentary trust: ■ Specific bequest/devise ■ Residuary bequest of personalty ■ Residuary devise of realty ■ Pecuniary legacy	Yes No, if postponed to a future date (*Re McGeorge*) Arguably carries intermediate income by virtue of s 175 of the LPA Only in situations outlined in 3(iii), above

pay it to IB's parents or guardians for this purpose. Where they do so, they must ensure that it is properly applied by the parents/guardians: see *Wilson v Turner* [1883].

Maintenance by court order: In addition to the trustee's power under s 31 to maintain an IB out of income, s 53 empowers the court to order the sale of trust property to which the IB is entitled with a view to applying the capital for his maintenance.

Moreover, where the power of maintenance in s 31 is excluded by the terms of the trust, the court may order the trust to be varied in order to allow maintenance: see *Re Collins* [1886].

The power of advancement

What is advancement? According to Viscount Radcliffe in *Pilkington v IRC* [1964], advancement 'means any use of money that will improve the material situation of the beneficiary'.

Broadly speaking, advancement entails making provision out of trust capital towards establishing a beneficiary in life before he becomes entitled to demand such capital. For example:

- buying the beneficiary an Army commission: see *Lawrie v Bankes* [1857];

- buying a house for doctor-beneficiary: see *Re Williams WT* [1953];

- paying off beneficiary's debts: see *Lowther v Bentinck* [1874];

- assisting the beneficiary to emigrate: see *Re Long's Settlement* [1868]; or start a career at the Bar: *Roper-Curzon v Roper-Curzon* [1871]; or set up in business: *Re Kershaw* [1868];

- paying medical and nursing home expenses of the elderly and infirm beneficiary out of capital: see *Stevenson v Wishart* [1987];

- redistributing trust capital under a resettlement which confers tax savings on the beneficiary: see *Pilkington v IRC* [1964].

The statutory power of advancement (s 32): An express power of advancement may be given to trustees in the trust instrument. If not, they may avail themselves of the statutory power in s 32 of the TA 1925 unless there is a contrary intention in the trust instrument.

Under s 32, the power of advancement is exercisable in favour of a beneficiary with an interest in trust capital, whether this is:

- an absolute vested interest: in this connection, the power of advancement is typically exercisable where a beneficiary is precluded from claiming the capital as of right because he is an infant or because another beneficiary has a prior right to the income;

- a vested interest which is liable to be defeated (for example, by the exercise of a power of appointment);

- a contingent interest; or

■ an interest which is subject to a gift over if the beneficiary dies under a specified age or some other event occurs.

Section 32 contemplates that any capital money advanced may be applied by the trustees themselves or paid to the beneficiary. Where the money is paid to the beneficiary, the trustees cannot stand back and leave it open to him to spend the money as he chooses but must seek to ensure that he applies it to the designated purpose: see *Re Pauling's ST* [1963].

Conditions for exercising the power of advancement in s 32:

(a) The sum advanced must not exceed one half of the vested or presumptive share or interest of the beneficiary in the property. The effect of this can be seen in the following illustrations:

  (i)   assuming that T holds £10,000 on trust for B if he attains the age of 21, T may advance up to £5,000 to B;

  (ii) if it happens that T holds £10,000 on trust for B1 and B2, who are both infants, in equal shares, each may be advanced up to £2,500;

  (iii) it might happen that T holds £12,000 on trust to be divided among all X's sons who are called to the Bar by the age of 30 and X dies leaving four sons under 30, T may advance £1,500 to each son;

  (iv) a situation might arise in which B receives one half of his presumptive share and thereafter the half still held by T rises appreciably in value. For example, B's presumptive share may be valued at £100,000 out of which he is advanced £50,000 in 2004. The £50,000 left in T's hand may become worth £70,000 in 2007, thus increasing the total value of B's entitlement to £120,000. *Abergavenny v Ram* [1982] establishes that B cannot receive an additional advancement of £10,000 to reflect the fact that half of his presumptive share is now £60,000, since T is deemed to have exhausted his power of advancement in 2004.

(b) Where B becomes entitled to receive his share of trust property after an advancement has been made in his favour, the sum advanced will be taken into account as part of his share.

(c) The power will not be exercisable to the prejudice of any person entitled to a prior life or other interest, unless such person is of full age and consents in writing to the advancement (as happened in *Pilkington v IRC*).

Note that, if this prior interest arises under a protective trust, and the principal beneficiary gives his consent to the exercise of the power of appointment, this will not operate to determine his interest under the protective trust.

Advancement by court order: The courts have established in cases like *Barlow v Grant* [1684] and *Re Mary England* [1830] that they have an inherent jurisdiction to order payments by way of advancement or maintenance out of the trust capital.

The power of delegation

Traditionally, trustees were considered to be under an obligation to perform their functions personally and not to delegate these functions unless this was provided for by the trust instrument. The operative principle in this regard was *delegatus non potest delegare*: see, for example, *Turner v Corney* [1841].

Where the trust instrument was silent, the courts recognised that delegation could take place within certain well-defined limits:

- firstly, delegation was permitted only where this was justified by legal necessity or ordinary business practice: see *Ex p Belcher* [1754] and *Speight v Gaunt* [1883];

- secondly, the trustee could delegate only his ministerial duties and not his discretions: see *Fry v Tapson* [1884];

- thirdly, the trustee was required to take reasonable care not only to appoint a competent agent but also to supervise him properly: see *Matthew v Brise* [1845]; *Rowland v Witherden* [1851]; and *Fry v Tapson*.

The scope for delegation by trustees has now been widened considerably by a number of statutory provisions:

- s 11 of the Trustee Act 2000 grants trustees the power to employ agents. Of particular relevance is s 15 which provides that trustees may authorise an agent to exercise their asset management functions as long as an agreement is in place, in or evidenced in writing. They must also prepare a statement that gives guidance as to how the function should be exercised ('a policy statement');

- s 17 of the Trustee Act 2000 makes provision for trustees to appoint custodians for the safe custody of the assets or of any documents or records concerning the assets;

- s 19 of the 2000 Act sets out the persons who may be appointed as nominees or custodians. Primarily, two main categories are favoured by the Act: those who carry on a business as nominees or custodians, and those who are corporate bodies controlled by the trustees;

- s 22 of the Trustee Act 2000 makes provision for the review of agents, nominees and custodians. Primarily, the trustees are required to keep under review the arrangements under which the agent, nominee or custodian acts (s 22(1)(a));

- a trustee is not liable for any act or default of the agent, nominee or custodian unless he has failed to comply with the duty of care applicable (s 23(1));

- s 32 makes provision for remuneration and expenses of agents, nominees and custodians out of the trust fund.

Delegation of trustee's functions by means of powers of attorney: Section 25 of the TA 1925 authorises a trustee to delegate the exercise of all or any of his functions (that is, duties/powers/discretions). To this end, he must execute a power of attorney and must also give written notice to his co-trustees and any person empowered to appoint new trustees.

Various conditions were inserted into s 25 to prevent excessive delegation by trustees. In particular:

- a trustee would only be allowed to delegate his functions for up to 12 months at a time;

- a trustee could only delegate under the original s 25 if he was leaving the UK for up to one month. This restriction has now been removed by the Powers of Attorney Act 1971;

- under the original s 25, delegation by one trustee to a co-trustee was not permitted where there were no other trustees. Section 25 has now been amended in several respects by the Trustee Delegation Act 1999. One such amendment enables delegation to a sole co-trustee;

▓ s 25(3) stipulated that the power of attorney had to be signed by the donor and attested by at least one witness. This requirement is now covered by s 1(3) of the Law of Property (Miscellaneous Provisions) Act 1989 and s 25(3) has accordingly been omitted from the amended version of s 25 contained in the 1999 Act.

In addition to the foregoing, s 9 of TLATA 1996 empowers trustees of land to delegate their functions in relation to land to any beneficiary who is of full age and entitled in possession. This may be done for any length of time and must be by means of a non-enduring power of attorney.

In the exercise of such delegated functions, the beneficiary will be liable in the same manner as a trustee. For their part, the delegating trustees shall not be liable for beneficiary's defaults unless they failed to take reasonable care in carrying out the delegation.

OTHER POWERS

These include:

▓ the power to sell trust property: see, for example, s 16 of the TA 1925; ss 1 and 67 of the Settled Land Act 1925; and s 130(1) of the LPA 1925;

▓ the power to issue receipts: see, for example, s 14(1) of the TA 1925. Where the receipt relates to the sale of land, it must be issued by at least two trustees except in the case of a trust corporation;

▓ the power to insure trust property: see, for example, s 19 of the TA 1925, as amended by s 34 of the Trustee Act 2000;

▓ the power to compound liabilities: see, for example, s 15 of the TA 1925;

▓ it is also noteworthy that, where a trust of land is concerned, it is expressly provided by s 6 of TLATA 1996 that, for the purpose of exercising their functions, the trustees shall have in relation to the trust land all the powers of an absolute owner.

VARIATION OF TRUSTS

Trustees must carry out the trust according to the express terms set out in the trust instrument as supplemented by the various implied terms imposed by statute.

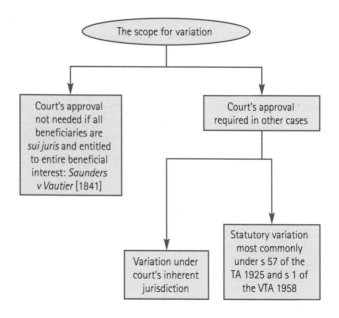

EXAM ISSUE: If the beneficiaries wish to vary the terms of the trust, they may invoke the rule in *Saunders v Vautier* [1841] which empowers them to end the trust and reconstitute it under whatever new terms they wish, provided they are all *sui juris* and hold the entirety of the beneficial interest in the trust property.

Where the rule in *Saunders v Vautier* does not avail the beneficiaries, any proposed variation must be sanctioned by the court either under its inherent jurisdiction or on the strength of powers conferred by various statutes.

VARIATION UNDER THE COURT'S INHERENT JURISDICTION

Over the years, the courts have in the exercise of their inherent jurisdiction sanctioned variations of trusts in a limited number of situations outlined in *Chapman v Chapman* [1954]:

■ where the trust instrument directed income to be accumulated in favour of an infant beneficiary without providing for his maintenance, the court could order such maintenance: see *Re Collins* [1866];

▓ where an unexpected emergency posed a serious threat to the trust, the court could enlarge the trustee's administrative powers to deal with it: see *Re Jackson* [1882]; *Re New* [1901]; and *Re Tollemache* [1903];

▓ where a dispute arose regarding the entitlement of beneficiaries under the trust, the courts sometimes sanctioned a compromise which ostensibly settled the dispute but in reality was designed to vary the beneficial interests as set out in the trust instrument. Significantly, in *Chapman*, the House of Lords declined to sanction a variation under this heading because it found that there was no genuine dispute to be compromised.

VARIATIONS AUTHORISED BY STATUTE

(a) Section 57 of the TA 1925 provides that where, in the management or administration of trust property, it becomes expedient to sell, lease, mortgage or otherwise dispose of such property or to undertake any purchase, investment, acquisition, transfer or other transaction but the trustees have no power to do so under the trust instrument or by law, the court may confer the necessary power on them.

The requirement that there had to be an emergency before additional administrative powers could be conferred under the court's inherent jurisdiction has been dispensed with under s 57 of the TA 1925.

The section has been invoked to confer additional powers on trustees in various contexts, for example:

Case	Nature of power conferred
Mason v Farbrother [1983]; *Anker-Petersen v Anker-Petersen* [1991]	To widen existing power to invest
Re Power [1947]	To purchase a home for beneficiaries
Re Beale's Settlement Trust [1932]	To enable sale of trust land
Re Hope [1929]	To enable sale of settled chattels
Re Cockerell's ST [1956]	To enable sale of residuary estate

It must, however, be noted that s 57 applies only where a proposed variation is intended to enlarge the administrative or managerial functions of the trustees and not where it is intended to redefine or refashion the beneficial interests created by the trust: see *Re Downshire's Settled Estates* [1953].

(b) The Variation of Trusts Act (VTA) 1958 was enacted in response to the House of Lords' refusal to exercise its compromise jurisdiction and approve the proposed variation in *Chapman*. The VTA 1958 empowers the court to not only enlarge the trustee's powers to administer trust property but also to approve arrangements varying or revoking all or any of the terms of the trust (including those relating to the interests of beneficiaries). As Lord Evershed MR declared in *Re Steed's WT* [1960], the Act has given the judges 'a very wide and indeed revolutionary discretion', in that it now enables them to sanction variations to the terms of a trust in instances where they would previously have felt unable to do so either on the basis of their inherent jurisdiction or under s 57 of the TA 1925. In *D (a child) v O* [2004], a scheme was approved to apply more than 50 per cent of the capital of the fund for the claimant's education.

VARIATION OF TRUSTS ACT 1958 – FOUR CLASSES OF BENEFICIARY

Under the VTA 1958, the court may approve proposed variations on behalf of four categories of persons, namely:

(a) Any person who is *unborn*, for example, a trust in favour of A for life remainder to A's eldest son where A as yet has no son. But, note *Re Pettifor's WT* [1966] which indicates that where there is little possibility of any such person being born (for example, a trust in favour of F for life, remainder to her children where F is 70 and childless) the trustee may deal with the trust property on the footing that F will bear no child in the future instead of seeking judicial approval for a variation under the VTA 1958.

(b) Any person who is an *infant* or who is *incapable of assenting to the variation because of some other incapacity*: see, for example, *Re Whittall* [1973] and *Re CL* [1969].

(c) Any person who has a *discretionary interest under a protective trust*, provided the interest of the principal beneficiary has not been determined.

(d) Any person (whether ascertained or not) who may become entitled to an interest as being at a future date or on the occurrence of a future event a person of a specified description or a member of a designated class, eg:

- where property is held on trust for A, remainder to his wife, and A is a bachelor, the court may approve a variation on behalf of any future wife he may marry: see *Re Clitheroe* [1959];
- where property is held on trust for A for life, remainder to his next-of-kin and A is still alive, the court may approve a variation on behalf of the next-of-kin: see *Re Moncrieff's ST* [1962].

Note, however, with regard to this fourth category, that the court cannot approve a variation on behalf of any person who would fit the description or would be a member of the designated class if the date had arrived or the event had occurred on the day the application was made to the court. For example, if property is held on trust for A for life remainder to his next-of-kin and A's cousin, C, is the person who would qualify as A's next-of-kin if A was dead on the day the application to vary the trust was made, C must consent to the variation and the court cannot do so on his behalf: see *Re Suffert* [1961].

Benefit

Where a proposed variation is presented to the court for approval on behalf of persons in categories (a), (b) and (d) (but not category (c)), it must be established that it is for the benefit of such persons.

Usually, it is sufficient to show that there will be some financial benefit such as tax savings: see, for example, *Re Druce's ST* [1962]; *Re Sainsbury's Settlement* [1967]; and *Gibbon v Mitchell* [1990].

In *Ridgwell v Ridgwell* [2007] the court approved a variation sought by trustees to create a life interest in the income of a trust fund valued at approximately £54 million on the death of the life tenant, Anthony Ridgwell, in favour of his spouse. Although this variation would defer the date when his children obtained a vested interest in the trust fund, the trustees would have a longer period in which to make advances to the children with consequent inheritance tax savings, and might also make savings in relation to capital gains tax and life insurance, which would far outweigh the disadvantage of the postponement of the children's interest in remainder.

The courts have, however, made it clear in cases like *Re Weston's Settlement* [1968]; *Re Holt's Settlement* [1969]; and *Re CL* [1969] that benefit in the present context is not confined to financial gain, but may extend to moral or social benefit. In *Weston*, for instance, the court refused to approve a proposed variation of the terms of the trust intended to enable the transfer of trust assets from settlements based in England to off-shore settlements in Jersey. While this arrangement would have produced considerable savings in tax, it would have meant that the settlor's children, on whose behalf approval was sought, would have had to move from England to Jersey which in the court's view was not for their overall benefit. Contrast this with *Re Seale's Marriage Settlement* [1961].

The weight to be accorded to the settlor's intention

The courts must not only ensure that the proposed variation is of benefit to those on whose behalf approval is sought but must enquire whether it runs counter to the settlor's intention. As Evershed MR explained in *Re Steed's WT* [1960], the court will 'look at the scheme as a whole and when it does so consider, as surely it must, what really was the intention of the benefactor'.

However, the Court of Appeal has since decided in *Goulding v James* [1997] that the settlor's intention is material only in determining whether a proposed variation is of benefit to the beneficiaries on whose behalf *judicial* approval is sought. If the variation is undoubtedly beneficial to them, the court will not oppose it simply because it does not reflect the settlor's intention. See also: *Knocker v Youle* [1986].

Position where adult beneficiary has not consented to variation

The general scheme of the VTA 1958 is to secure the consent of all the beneficiaries to the proposed variation with those who are ascertained and who possess the requisite capacity consenting for themselves and the court doing likewise for those not in a position to consent for themselves.

Accordingly, where an adult beneficiary (not being one on whose behalf the court can give approval under s 1) has not consented to a proposed variation the court may adjourn proceedings until his consent is obtained. Such consent is necessary even if the beneficiary merely has a contingent interest which has little prospect of vesting (as in *Knocker v Youle* [1986]). If the court mistakenly approves a variation without the requisite consent, it appears from *IRC v Holmden* [1968] that the non-consenting beneficiary is not bound by it and may seek an injunction to prevent the trustees from departing from the original terms of the trust.

You should now be confident that you would be able to tick all of the boxes on the checklist at the beginning of this chapter. To check your knowledge of Trustees and administration of the trusts why not visit the companion website and take the Multiple Choice Question test. Check your understanding of the terms and vocabulary used in this chapter with the flashcard glossary.

11

Breach of trust and remedies

When does a breach of trust occur?

What is the liability of incoming and retired trustees?

What are the implications of joint liability of trustees?

What is the measure of a trustee's liability for breach of trust?

What are the defences to an action for personal liability?

How are exemption clauses in the trust instrument treated?

When is a claim statute barred?

What is the distinction between tracing and following?

What conditions must be satisfied for equitable tracing?

Discuss tracing into unmixed funds

Explain tracing when the trust fund is mixed with the trustee's funds

Discuss tracing into two trust funds which have been mixed together

Can tracing take place when trust funds have been paid to an innocent volunteer?

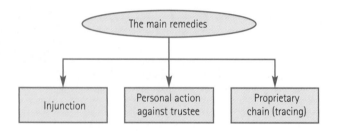

A breach of trust occurs where a trustee fails to perform any of his duties or improperly exercises any of his powers. The beneficiaries may proceed against a trustee who commits a breach even where the trustee believed that what he was doing was in the best interest of the trust: see *Re Brogden* [1888]; unless his act or omission constitutes a mere technical breach which the court would have authorised if leave been sought: see *Lee v Brown* [1798] and *Brown v Smith* [1878].

INJUNCTION

This remedy is available to prevent anticipated breaches, for example:

Case	Purpose of injunction
Dance v Goldingham [1873]	To restrain unauthorised sale
Riggal v Foster [1853]	To restrain unnecessary mortgage
Fox v Fox [1870]	To prevent improper distribution

THE PERSONAL REMEDY

Where a breach has in fact been committed by a trustee, he will be personally liable to the beneficiaries for any benefit which he receives as a result as well as any loss suffered by the trust.

A trustee will not, however, be vicariously liable for the breaches of co-trustees or the dishonesty or neglect of agents who act for the trust, unless there has been wilful default on his part, as happened in *Townley v Sherborne* [1634] where a trustee was affixed with liability for allowing rents collected on trust property to remain in the hands of his co-trustee who misapplied the money. More recently, in *Segbedzi v Segbedzi* [1999], a trustee who by his own neglect allowed his fellow trustees to sell the principal asset of the trust at an under-value was held liable even though he did not participate actively in the breach. See also *Re Lucking's WT* [1968]; ss 22 and 23 of the Trustee Act 2000 in respect of keeping delegates under review.

LIABILITY OF INCOMING AND RETIRED TRUSTEES

As a rule, an incoming trustee is not liable for breaches committed by his pred-ecessors but, if he becomes aware of such a breach after assuming office, he must take steps to remedy it: see *Re Strahan* [1856].

A retired trustee will, for his part, be liable for breaches he committed while in office but not for breaches committed by other trustees after his departure, unless his retirement was intended to pave the way for the commission of the breach in question: see *Head v Gould* [1898].

JOINT LIABILITY

Where two or more trustees are involved in committing a breach, their liability is *joint and several* and the beneficiaries may sue all or any of them.

If any one trustee is sued, he may claim a *contribution* from any other trustee who is also liable. Originally, equity required each trustee to make an equal contribution, but under the Civil Liability (Contribution) Act 1978, the courts are now able to set the level of each trustee's contribution to reflect the extent of his responsibility for the breach.

Where two trustees are jointly liable for a breach, one may be able to claim an *indemnity* from the other. In particular:

- An indemnity may be claimed against a solicitor-trustee by his co-trustee who has placed complete reliance on the solicitor in the affairs of the trust (see *Chillingworth v Chambers* [1896]; *Re Linsley* [1904]) but not by a co-trustee who, acting on his own judgment, has actively participated: see *Head v Gould* [1898].

■ An indemnity may also be claimed by a trustee against his co-trustee where the latter has acted fraudulently in initiating the breach (see *Re Smith* [1896]) but not where the trustee claiming the indemnity has simply abdicated his responsibilities and the breach is occasioned by the honest but erroneous actions of his co-trustee: see *Bahin v Hughes* [1886].

THE MEASURE OF A TRUSTEE'S LIABILITY

Once a breach of trust is established it becomes necessary to determine the extent of the trustee's liability. This is usually done by reference to the profit which he made or the loss occasioned to the trust estate by the breach. In *Target Holdings v Redferns* [1994], the Court of Appeal went so far as to hold that the obligation to make good the loss arising from a breach remained even if that loss would have been incurred without the breach. This was, however, rejected on appeal by the House of Lords which held that a trustee's liability to make good a breach was fault based. As such, the solicitor-trustee in this case would be liable only if the loss would not have been incurred had it not been for the breach.

The courts have been called upon to determine the liability of trustees in a variety of contexts. The following rules have emerged from their judicial pronouncements:

■ A trustee who makes an unauthorised investment is liable to pay the difference between the cost of the investment and the price at which it is sold: see *Knott v Cottee* [1852].

■ If all the beneficiaries are of full age, it has been accepted in cases like *Wright v Morgan* [1926] that they may choose, instead, to adopt the investment. If they do so, but its value has fallen below the price the trustees paid for it, some cases (for example, *Thornton v Stokill* [1855]) suggest that they cannot recover the difference; whereas other cases (for example, *Re Lake* [1903]) suggest they can.

■ A trustee who improperly retains an unauthorised investment will be liable to pay the difference between the price at which it is sold (or its value at the judgment date if not sold) and what it would have fetched if it had been sold at the appropriate time: see *Fry v Fry* [1859]. In *Jeffrey v Gretton* [2011] trustees were in breach of their duty to regularly review the trust portfolio when they failed to take professional advice and decided to keep a valuable but dilapidated property and refurbish it rather than sell it. The method for calculating compensation was to compare the value of the property at the date on which a sale should have taken place in 2002 with the value when it was actually sold in 2008. In fact, in the present case, that calculation showed that the beneficiaries had suffered no loss.

■ A trustee who improperly sells an authorised investment may either be required to replace it or pay the difference between the price at which it was sold and what it will cost to replace it: see *Re Bell's Indenture* [1980].

■ If a trustee, having improperly sold an authorised investment, invests the proceeds in an unauthorised security and later sells this security for no less than it was bought, he will still be liable for the difference between this amount and the prevailing value of the authorised investment originally held by him. In *Re Massingberd's ST* [1890], it was held that the value of the authorised investment should be determined by reference to the replacement cost at the date the writ was issued; while in *Re Bell's Indenture* it was suggested that it should be the replacement cost at the judgment date. In *Jaffray v Marshall* [1994], the court after reviewing both cases signified that it should be the highest intermediate value of the asset between the date of the breach and the judgment date.

■ Trustees must invest trust funds without undue delay. In the case of a trustee who is merely under a general duty to invest, any undue delay in investing simply renders him liable to pay interest on the uninvested fund. See *Shepherd v Mouls* [1845].

The position is different where the trustee is required by the trust instrument to invest in one type of asset but delays unduly and the cost of the asset increases in the meantime. Cases like *Byrchall v Bradford* [1822] and *Pride v Fooks* [1840] suggest that he will be liable for the difference between what it would have cost to invest at the appropriate time and the increased value of the asset. It was, however, held in *Robinson v Robinson* [1851] that, where the trustee is given a choice between two investments and delays unduly in selecting one, it is the value of the investment which has performed less favourably that will be used in determining the trustee's liability. This proposition did not find favour with Dillon LJ, who argued in *Nestlé v National Westminster Bank* [1993] that, in such an event, the trustees ought to pay a 'fair compensation' for failing to follow a proper investment policy: the so-called 'portfolio theory'.

- Trustees cannot ordinarily set off a profit made from one transaction against a loss from another transaction entered into in breach of trust (see *Dimes v Scott* [1828] and *Wills v Gresham* [1854]) except where the profit and loss resulted from the same transaction or the same policy decision to pursue a particular course of investment: see *Bartlett v Barclays Bank Trust Co (No 1)* [1980].

- Once the extent of the trustee's liability is determined, interest will usually be charged on the sum due from the date of the breach. For a long time, the rate of interest was set at 4 per cent (or 5 per cent in the case of a fraudulent breach) but, nowadays, interest is usually awarded in line with prevailing commercial rates: see, for example, *Wallersteiner v Moir (No 2)* [1975]; *Belmont Finance v Williams Furniture (No 2)* [1980]; and *Guardian Ocean Cargoes v Banco do Brasil (No 3)* [1994].

▶ BARTLETT v BARCLAYS [1980]

Basic facts

A settlement consisted of all the debenture stock and shares in a private company. The bank was the trustee of the settlement. The bank did not attend the company's monthly meetings, and without the bank's knowledge the company embarked on two very hazardous property deals. By luck one project succeeded, and the proceeds were used to invest in the other project. It failed, and the company suffered a large loss. The only information the bank had had throughout was gleaned at annual general meetings. The beneficiaries took proceedings against the bank for breach of trust.

Held, that a prudent businessman would not have been content only with the information from annual general meetings in the conduct of his own affairs. Moreover, the bank, as a professional corporate trustee owed a higher duty of care, and was liable for loss caused by failure to exercise the special care and skill which it professed to have. The bank was therefore liable for the project loss. They could, however, set off the profit resulting from the first project, since it arose from the same speculation policy.

Relevance

Where a trustee, such as a trust corporation, held itself out as having the skill and expertise to carry on the specialised business of trust management, the duty of care of such a trustee was higher than the standard of care of the ordinary prudent man of business as demanded of a trustee without specialised knowledge.

A trustee will be allowed to 'set off' losses and profits made *only* when part of the same transaction.

DEFENCES TO AN ACTION FOR PERSONAL LIABILITY

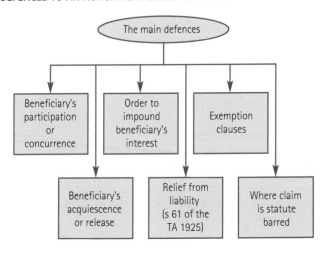

(1) The beneficiary's participation or concurrence in a breach

A trustee has a defence against a beneficiary who participates in or consents to a breach even if the latter derived no benefit. To rely on this defence, the trustee must show that the beneficiary acted of his own free will and understood what he was doing: see *Re Pauling's WT* [1963] and *Holder v Holder* [1968].

This defence cannot be raised against any beneficiary apart from the one who participated/concurred in the breach: see *Fletcher v Collis* [1905].

> ▶ Re PAULING'S ST [1961]

Relevance
Trustee's duty to supervise advancements – may be liable for breach where consenting beneficiary under undue influence.

(2) Acquiescence or release by beneficiary

A trustee will also have a good defence against a beneficiary who learns of a breach after its commission and then releases the trustee from liability or otherwise acquiesces in the breach: see *Walker v Symonds* [1818]; *Farrant v Blanchford* [1863]; and *Re Garnett* [1885].

(3) Impounding the beneficiary's interest

Where a breach is committed at the instigation or with the consent of a beneficiary, the court may order that his interest should be impounded and applied towards repairing the breach either under its inherent jurisdiction or under s 62 of the Trustee Act (TA) 1925.

Inherent jurisdiction:

■ where a breach is requested/instigated by the beneficiary, his interest can be impounded whether or not he benefited from it: see *Trafford v Boehm* [1746]; *Fuller v Knight* [1843]; and *Chillingworth v Chambers* [1896];

■ where the beneficiary merely consented, his interest will be impounded only where he benefited from the breach: see *Booth v Booth* [1838] and *Chillingworth v Chambers* [1896].

Section 62 of the TA 1925: Authorises a beneficiary's interest to be impounded in the event of a breach whether he benefited from it or not:

■ where the beneficiary instigated the breach; or

■ where he consented *in writing* to the commission of the breach.

Note, however, that a beneficiary's interest will not be impounded if he asks the trustees to perform an act which is not in itself a breach but the act is carried out by them in a manner which gives rise to a breach: see *Re Somerset* [1894].

(4) Relief from liability under s 61 of the TA 1925

Such relief is available at the court's discretion where a trustee has committed a breach but in so doing has acted honestly and reasonably such that it would be fair to excuse him from liability.

As explained by Byrne J in *Re Turner* [1897], the courts have not sought to lay down strict rules for deciding whether to grant relief but are guided by the circumstances of each case.

Cases in which the courts were prepared to grant relief include:

- *Perrins v Bellamy* [1899]: where trustees sold leaseholds belonging to the trust on the erroneous advice of their solicitors;

- *Re De Clifford* [1900]: where trust money entrusted by trustees to a solicitor in good faith to defray trust expenses was lost on the solicitor's bankruptcy; and

- *Evans v Westcombe* [1999]: where a personal representative had, on legal advice, taken out an insurance policy in favour of a missing beneficiary who later reappeared and brought a claim for an account and lost interest in respect of his share of the estate.

By contrast, cases in which such relief was refused include *Re Barker* [1898], where a trustee, on the advice of a commission agent, improperly retained unauthorised investments for 14 years.

(5) EXAM ISSUE: Exemption clauses in trust instruments

Exemption clauses are express provisions in a trust instrument which exonerate trustees from acts/omissions that would otherwise constitute breaches of trust. They are often found in professional trustees' terms of business and afford a trustee a good defence whenever he is sued in respect of any breach which comes within the ambit of the clause. They are usually framed in very wide terms, as typified by cl 15 of the trust instrument in the leading case of *Armitage v Nurse* [1998]. In that case it was stated that 'No trustees shall be liable for any loss or damage which may happen to the trust fund ... at any time or from any cause whatsoever unless such loss shall be caused by his own actual fraud'.

The extent of the immunity given by such widely framed exemption clauses has been a source of contention among academic commentators and has also preoccupied the courts in recent cases.

One matter on which there is more or less universal agreement is that, however widely framed an exemption clause, it cannot exclude a trustee's liability for a breach involving *fraud* or *dishonesty*. The reason for this, as explained by Hayton in his essay on 'The irreducible core content of trusteeship' (and affirmed by Millett LJ in *Armitage*) is that the trustee's duty to act in good faith is a core obligation which is fundamental to the trust and this duty cannot be excluded by a clause which purports to exempt the trustee from liability for dishonesty/ fraud.

In *Bonham v Fishwick* [2008], the court considered whether the respondent trustees (alleged to have committed wilful and individual wrongdoing) were entitled to rely on an exemption clause in the trust instrument which exempted them from liability for breach of trust except in the case of 'wilful and individual fraud or wrongdoing'. The court held that the allegation against the trustees was not arguable as the trustees had heeded the legal advice given by their counsel and solicitor when acting and accordingly were entitled to rely in their defence on the trustee exemption clause.

A further issue which has arisen is whether a trustee can rely on an exemption clause where a breach of trust is caused by his negligence. There is a broad consensus in academic circles that exempting liability for negligence is undesirable, especially where the exemption is being invoked by a professional trustee who has been retained and is being remunerated for his expertise and whose acts and omissions would otherwise constitute professional negligence.

Despite such legitimate concerns, the prevailing judicial position is that, where an exemption clause is framed in such wide terms as that in *Armitage*, it is capable of exonerating a trustee from liability for his breaches of trust even where he is guilty of *gross negligence*. As Millett LJ put it in this case, such a trustee would not be liable for any loss or damage unless caused by his dishonesty, no matter how indolent, imprudent, lacking in diligence, negligent or wilful he might have been. He maintained that an exclusion clause which had this effect was not repugnant to the concept of a trust, since the trustee's core obligations did not, in his view, include the duties of skill and care, prudence and diligence. The position espoused by Millett LJ was reaffirmed in *Bogg v Raper* [1998] and *Wight v Olswang* [1999], but this was tempered by the tendency shown by the court in both cases to construe the relevant exemption clauses as restrictively as the wording would permit against the trustees who sought to rely on them.

EXAM ISSUE: Note that these judgments predate the statutory duty of care introduced by s 1 of the Trustee Act 2000. Until there are decided cases on the application of s 1, it is not clear whether the preceding cases will still be considered good law. It seems likely, however, that the courts will still recognise the distinction between 'core obligations' and contractual obligations in relation to trustees' duties.

The Law Commission published a report on Trustee Exemption Clauses in 2006. The Law Commission decided against recommending legislation as this has received little support during the consultation process, and restricted the autonomy of a settlor.

Instead it was proposed that professional or regulatory bodies (such as the Law Society) should provide statements of best practice under which their members (ie professional trustees) would be required to bring any exclusion clause inserted in the trust instrument which excluded or limited their liability for negligence to the attention of the settlor. This would ensure that the settlor was aware of the effect of the exclusion clause.

However, the Law Commission's stance has been criticised since it does not impose a legal obligation on trustees to control exclusion clauses in the trust instrument, although a breach of the statement of best practice would probably lead to disciplinary action being taken against the trustee.

(6) Statute barred claims
Various limitation periods are prescribed by statute for different types of action. Thus, s 21(3) of the Limitation Act 1980 lays down the general rule that an action for breach of trust must be commenced not more than six years from the date on which the cause of action accrued. If the action is commenced outside the six year period, the trustee may claim in his defence that it is statute barred unless the action:

■ is for fraud or a fraudulent breach of trust to which the trustee is party or privy. In *Gwembe Valley Development Co Ltd v Koshy and Others* [2003], the court decided that no limitation period applied to a claim for an account because of the fraudulent conduct of the trustee in receiving unauthorised profits, or

■ is to recover trust property or its proceeds in the trustee's hands or previously received by him and converted to his use.

EXAM ISSUE: THE PROPRIETARY PROCESS OF TRACING

The distinction between tracing, following, and claiming

To explain why this is important, we must go back to Lord Millett's speech in *Foskett*, where he distinguished between tracing, following, and claiming – not because the Jersey law in this area is necessarily the same as the English law, but because one cannot meaningfully compare the two without first establishing a stable definition of what these terms mean. Lord Millett held as follows –

> [Tracing and following] are both exercises in locating assets which are or may be taken to represent an asset belonging to the plaintiffs and to which they assert ownership. The processes of following and tracing are, however, distinct. Following is the process of following the same asset as it moves from hand to hand. Tracing is the process of identifying a new asset as the substitute for the old. Where one asset is exchanged for another, a claimant can elect whether to follow the original asset into the hands of the new owner or to trace its value into the new asset in the hands of the same owner. . . . Tracing is also distinct from claiming. It identifies the traceable proceeds of the claimant's property. It enables the claimant to substitute the traceable proceeds for the original asset as the subject matter of his claim. But it does not affect or establish his claim. That will depend on a number of factors including the nature of his interest in the original asset. He will normally be able to maintain the same claim to the substituted asset as he could have maintained to the original asset. . . . But his claim may also be exposed to potential defences as a result of intervening transactions.

In the words of another English judge, Moore-Bick J, Lord Millett therefore understood 'the rules of following and tracing . . . [to be] essentially evidential in nature', and he considered them to be essentially distinct from 'rules which determine substantive rights: the former are concerned with identifying property in other hands or in another form; the latter with the rights that a claimant can assert against the property in its present form'.

This is available where a personal action will not suffice, eg where the trustee is insolvent. Tracing is a process whereby the claimant is given the opportunity to identify his property. This process may be followed up with a claim to assert a proprietary interest in the property. This claim may be pursued not only against a trustee who has committed the breach but also against any person to whom he has transferred trust property or assets in breach of trust. For example tracing would be available against a third party who had dishonestly received trust property following a breach of trust – see Chapter 6 – recipient liability.

Tracing is available both under the common law and in equity. In the present context, we are primarily concerned with the latter.

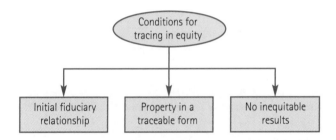

CONDITION 1: THERE MUST BE AN INITIAL FIDUCIARY RELATIONSHIP
The requirement was reaffirmed by Ferris J in *Box v Barclays Bank* [1998]:

> ... equitable tracing is only available where there is an equity to trace which requires that there must be an initial fiduciary relationship between the person claiming to trace and the party who is said to have misapplied that person's money.

This requirement is easily satisfied as between trustee and beneficiary not only where their relationship arises under an express trust but also where it arises under a resulting or constructive trust.

Moreover, several cases have affirmed that tracing orders may be made in relation to other types of fiduciary relationships, for example:

Case	Nature of fiduciary relationship
■ *Sinclair v Brougham* [1914]	Building society and its depositors: now overruled by the House of Lords in the *Westdeutsche Landesbank* case
■ *Re Diplock* [1948]	Executors and deceased's next-of-kin
■ *Chase Manhattan Bank v Israel-British Bank* [1979]	Relationship arising from mistaken overpayment by CMB to IBB
■ *Boscawen v Bajwa* [1995]	Relationship arising from advance of funds by bank as mortgagor to enable mortgagee to complete purchase of property which ultimately fell through

▶ Re DIPLOCK'S ESTATE [1948]

Basic facts

The executors of a deceased estate distributed it among 130 charitable institutions. Subsequently it was suggested, on behalf of persons interested as next of kin of the testator, that the gift was invalid. The charitable institutions were volunteers, having provided no value for the gifts that were made to them. The next-of-kin, having exhausted their remedies against the executors, successfully claimed the money back from the charities.

Relevance

Tracing allowed against innocent volunteers *unless* money used to improve property.

CONDITION 2: PROPERTY IN A TRACEABLE FORM

A tracing order would be futile, unless there is property to trace into. This depends ultimately on what the trustee does with the trust assets in his hands. In this regard, there are various possibilities.

Tracing into unmixed funds

■ Where the trust fund remains intact and is kept separately by the trustee (T), the beneficiary (B) is entitled to trace into the fund to the exclusion of T's other creditors.

■ Where T withdraws trust money and, without mixing it with his own, uses it to purchase a specific asset, B has a right to trace into the asset. This right entitles B either to claim the asset itself or to treat it as security for the trust money expended on the purchase: see *Re Hallett's Estate* [1880].

■ Where T withdraws and squanders trust money without mingling it with his own, B's right to trace in priority to T's other creditors is lost.

Tracing into trust funds which are mixed with trustee's funds

■ Where T becomes bankrupt after mixing trust funds with his own, B cannot trace into any part of the mixed fund in priority to T's other creditors, if the mixing was authorised by the terms of the trust: see *Space Investments v Canadian Imperial Bank of Commerce Trust* [1986]. If such mixing was done unlawfully, the extent of B's entitlement to trace depends on what thereafter happens to the mixed fund.

■ Where no withdrawals are made after mixing, B can lay claim to the part of the mixed fund derived from the trust in priority to T's other creditors: see *Re Hallett* [1880].

■ Where T withdraws the mixed fund and purchases specific property with it, it emerges from *Re Hallett* [1880], as well as *Sinclair v Brougham* [1914], that B obtains a first charge over the property purchased to the extent that trust money had been used to purchase it.

■ Should such property increase in value after the purchase, it was unclear whether B could claim a proportionate share of increased value. It appeared from *Re Hallett* [1880] and *Sinclair* that the charge which arose in B's favour in such circumstances covered only the amount of trust money put into the purchase and did not extend to the increased value of the property purchased. This issue was resolved in *Foskett v McKeown* [2000] where, by a majority of 3:2 in the House of Lords, it was held that the claimants, whose money was wrongly used to purchase at least two out of five premiums on a life policy, were entitled to a proportion of the policy proceeds and not just a charge over the proceeds to the amount of their contribution to the premium payments.

■ Where T withdraws part of the mixed fund and squanders it, *Re Hallett* establishes that he is deemed to have spent his own money first, with the result that B will have a prior claim to the balance in the mixed fund in order to recover what is due to the trust.

■ Where T, after mixing trust funds with his own, purchases property with part of the mixed fund and then squanders the balance, if T is deemed to have spent his own money first (as contemplated by the rule in *Re Hallett* [1880]) this would mean in effect that T's money was used to purchase the property while the trust money has been squandered. To avert such an outcome, *Re Oatway* [1903] decided that the rule in *Re Hallett* does not apply in the present context and affirmed that, in such circumstances, B will have a charge over the property purchased out of the mixed fund in priority to any other creditors of T.

■ The position is less clear cut where, after the mixing has occurred, T purchases an asset with part of the mixed fund but retains in the account a balance in excess of or equivalent to the trust money. Assuming the asset has since increased in value, can B lay claim to it? This matter was not specifically dealt with in *Re Oatway* [1903] where the whole balance was dissipated after the purchase. A combined reading of *Re Hallett* [1880] and *Re Tilley's WT* [1967], however, suggests that T will be presumed to have spent his own money first so that B's entitlement will be to trace into the balance rather than the asset purchased out of the mixed fund. EXAM ISSUE: Would it be possible to apply *Foskett v McKeown* here?

■ Where T has mixed trust money with his own funds then withdraws part of the mixed fund and later pays in additional money of his own, *Roscoe v Winder* [1915] established that B will only be able to trace into the *least intermediate balance* and thus has no priority over T's other creditors in respect of the additional payment. For example, T pays £1,000 of trust money into his account, which already contained £1,000 of his own money. T then withdraws £1,800, leaving a balance of £200. A week later, T pays £800 of his own money into the account. B can only trace into the £200.

▩ B's position is even more precarious where the account holding the mixed fund contains a zero balance or is overdrawn at the time of the subsequent payment of T's own money. This may occur for instance where:

(1) T, having paid £1,000 of trust money into his account which already contains £1,000 of his own money, later withdraws the entire £2,000, before paying in £800 of his own money;

(2) T's account is overdrawn by £1,500 when he pays £1,000 of trust money into it and he thereafter pays £800 of his own money into the same account.

Applying the principle in *Roscoe v Winder* [1915], the intermediate balance in situation (1) would be zero and, in situation (2), −£500, and so there will be nothing for B to trace into in either instance.

An alternative approach was put forward by Lord Templeman in the *Space Investment* case [1986]. Here, a bank-trustee had deposited trust funds in accounts it operated within the bank and was later wound up. Lord Templeman suggested that insofar as these deposits had helped to swell the bank's total assets, the beneficiaries ought to be entitled to trace the trust money into all the bank's assets, thus entitling them to a charge over all these assets. This would seem to suggest that, in the two situations referred to above, in so far as T's assets would have been swelled by the injection of £1,000 of trust money, B should be entitled to trace into any asset in the account (that is, the additional £800).

Commentators like Martin, however, insist that such an outcome is supported neither by principle nor by policy and would operate unfairly against T's other creditors. Moreover, although there has been no outright judicial repudiation of Lord Templeman's swollen assets theory, subsequent cases, such as *Bishopsgate Investment Management v Homan* [1994] and *Re Goldcorp* [1995] have sought to minimise its effect by emphasising that:

● Lord Templeman's pronouncement was made *obiter*;

● his Lordship was in fact concerned with tracing into a mixed fund as opposed to a non-existent fund such as an overdrawn account or one with a zero balance.

Both *Goldcorp* and *Homan* affirmed, in accordance with the principle in *Roscoe v Winder*, that, where such a non-existent fund is concerned, the beneficiary loses his right to trace. This was reinforced by *Re Lewis of Leicester* [1995] and *Box v Barclays Bank* [1998].

▨ *Backward tracing*: where T borrows money to purchase an asset and thereafter utilises trust funds to pay off the sum borrowed, the question arises as to whether this entitles B to trace into the asset. For example, T obtains an overdraft of £3,000 from his bank which he uses to buy a car. T then pays off the overdraft with £3,000 of trust money (leaving a zero balance). Can B claim priority over T's other creditors by tracing into the car? This issue was considered in *Homan* where there was a marked divergence of judicial opinion.

On the one hand, Vinelot J and, on appeal, Dillon LJ, recognised the possibility of such 'backward tracing' in certain narrowly defined circumstances, notably:

● where T acquired an asset with money borrowed from an overdrawn or loan account and there was an inference that the borrowing was done with the intention that it would be repaid with the misappropriated trust funds;

● where the misappropriated trust funds were paid into T's overdrawn account in order to reduce the overdraft and enable T to draw further sums from the account to purchase the asset.

On the other hand, Leggatt LJ refused to countenance a tracing claim in respect of an asset acquired before the misappropriation and hence without the aid of trust money.

▨ *Tracing and subrogation*: Where money is provided by T to discharge a debt owed to C, a secured creditor (for example, a mortgage debt) and the tracing process discloses that this was trust money, it was established in *Boscawen v Bajwa* [1995] that the right of subrogation is available to B. This entitles B to step into C's shoes and assert whatever proprietary right C might have over the asset which secured the debt.

Tracing into two trust funds which have become mixed together

▓ Where funds from two separate trust funds administered by the same trustee are mixed with his own funds, the rule in *Re Hallett's Estate* [1880] applies so that he is deemed to have spent his own money first.

▓ As between the two trust funds whose monies have been mixed, the position is determined primarily by reference to the rule in *Clayton's Case* [1816]. Under this rule, the first of the two trust funds to be paid into the account is deemed to have been withdrawn first, so that the beneficiaries under the second trust will be entitled to trace into the balance of the account in priority to the beneficiaries of the first trust. It was held, however, in *Barlow Clowes v Vaughan* [1992] that this 'first in-first out' rule is no more than a rule of convenience and will not be used to determine such competing claims where the court discovers a contrary intention, whether express or implied. In *Commerzbank Aktiengesellschaft v IMB Morgan* [2004], the court refused to apply the rule in *Clayton's Case* where its application would have led to injustice. Instead, the court applied the principle laid down in *Barlow Clowes and Russell-Cooke Trust Company v Prentis* [2003] to resolve competing claims to a fund by innocent customers. This approach found favour with the court in respect of unprofitable investments. The beneficiaries are to be treated as suffering a shared misfortune. Discuss *pari passu*?

▓ Where specific property is purchased with money from the mixed fund, both sets of beneficiaries will have a charge over the property purchased and will rank *pari passu* in proportion to the share of the purchase price derived from their respective trust funds: see *Sinclair v Brougham* [1914].

Tracing into trust funds which have been paid to innocent volunteers
EXAM ISSUE: Maxim: Equity will not assist a volunteer. It has been established in cases like *Re Diplock* that B's right to trace extends to situations where T transfers trust money or property to an innocent volunteer (V):

▓ Where the trust money remains intact or the trust property remains undisposed of in V's hands, B will have no difficulty in recovering it from him through the process of tracing.

▓ Where V sells such trust property after receiving it and keeps the proceeds separate from his own funds, B becomes entitled to trace into the proceeds.

▓ Where the trust money received by V (or the proceeds of the sale of trust property given to him) is mixed with V's own money and withdrawals are subsequently made from the mixed fund leaving a balance, the position of V and B, vis à vis this balance, is ordinarily determined by reference to the 'first in-first out rule' in *Clayton's Case*.

▓ Where property is subsequently purchased using the mixed fund, V and B will rank *pari passu* in their respective entitlements in accordance with the rule in *Sinclair v Brougham* [1914].

CONDITION 3: NO INEQUITABLE RESULTS

Like all equitable orders, a tracing order is discretionary and will not be awarded if, in the court's view, to do so would lead to inequitable results: see *Re Diplock* [1948].

Closely allied to the proposition that tracing will be disallowed if it produces inequitable results is the doctrine of change of position. The possible application of this doctrine in the sphere of tracing was acknowledged by the House of Lords in *Lipkin Gorman v Karpnale* [1991].

EXAM ISSUE: The effect of the doctrine in this sphere may well be that where V, acting in good faith, utilises trust money received by him in improving his own property or has committed himself to other expenditure which he would not have done if the trust money had not been available to him, the court can relieve him wholly or in part from his liability to make restitution to B.

You should now be confident that you would be able to tick all of the boxes on the checklist at the beginning of this chapter. To check your knowledge of Breach of trust and remedies why not visit the companion website and take the Multiple Choice Question test. Check your understanding of the terms and vocabulary used in this chapter with the flashcard glossary.

Equitable remedies of injunction and specific performance

What is an injunction?	
Compare a final injunction with an interim injunction	
What is the difference between a mandatory injunction and a prohibitory injunction?	
What is a *quia timet* injunction?	
Describe the general principles in granting a perpetual injunction	
What are the principles laid down in *American Cyanamid*?	
When will a freezing order be granted?	
What are the main characteristics of a search order?	
Describe an order for specific performance	
When will such an order not be granted?	

EQUITABLE REMEDIES

THE INJUNCTION

General principles

An injunction (broadly an order to do or refrain from doing something) is an equitable remedy and, as such, is granted at the discretion of the court, ie unlike damages, it is not available as of right.

It is used in many different situations, eg to restrain a breach of trust, to restrain the commission of a tort such as trespass to land or commission of a nuisance, to protect copyright, patent rights and trade marks, as a search order, or a freezing order.

It arises from the ability of equity to act *in personam*, ie against the wrongdoer's conscience. If the wrongdoer fails to comply with the injunction, this may result in contempt of court, the ultimate penalty for which is imprisonment. The High Court's jurisdiction to grant injunctions is found in s 37(1) of the Supreme Court Act 1981 which provides that 'the High Court may by order (whether interlocutory or final) grant an injunction ... in all cases in which it appears to the court to be just and convenient to do so.'

TYPES OF INJUNCTION

Perpetual injunction

A perpetual injunction is also called a final injunction and is granted when the court has heard the arguments of both sides and seeks to settle the dispute. It will not necessarily last for ever but it is final in that it resolves the dispute. It may be mandatory or prohibitory in nature – see below.

Interim injunction

In contrast to a perpetual injunction, an interim injunction (formerly referred to as an interlocutory injunction) is granted in order to maintain the status quo before the full hearing of the case has taken place. In other words, it is granted on an interim basis and is binding only up to the date of final judgment. It may be mandatory or prohibitory or a *quia timet* injunction – see below. There are two special types of interim injunction – the freezing order and the search order which are considered at the end of the section on injunctions.

Mandatory or prohibitory injunction

A mandatory injunction commands a person to perform a positive act. They are relatively rare because they are more draconian in effect particularly where a mandatory interim injunction is sought. Also in a contractual situation, they are similar to an order for specific performance and are subject to the same restrictions. For example, a mandatory injunction would not be ordered in respect of an act which involved continuous obligations on the part of the defendant because such an order would be difficult to supervise. A prohibitory injunction, as its name suggests, restrains or prohibits a person from doing a particular act.

A *quia timet* injunction

This is ordered to protect the claimant from an act which has not yet occurred but which it is feared may be committed in the future. *Quia timet* means literally 'he who fears'. There must be evidence of an immediate threat by the defendant to do something not simply a vague fear – see *Redland Bricks Ltd v Morris* [1970].

GENERAL PRINCIPLES IN GRANTING PERPETUAL INJUNCTIONS

The restrictions or conditions governing the grant of a perpetual injunction are similar to those governing an order for specific performance. Briefly, they are as follows:

Damages (or other legal remedies) are an inadequate remedy

Damages would not be an adequate remedy if money would not properly compensate the claimant as in the case of repeated nuisances, or if the defendant were insolvent. However, see below 'damages in lieu of an injunction'.

The conduct of the claimant is unconscionable

It is a characteristic of an equitable remedy that it will not be granted if the claimant has behaved inequitably. This is in accordance with the maxim 'He who comes to equity must come with clean hands' and 'He who comes to equity must do equity'. See *Hubbard v Vosper* [1972].

The claimant must not delay in seeking the injunction or acquiesce to the violation of his rights

Delay (known as laches) in seeking an injunction may lead to the court deciding not to grant an injunction. Delay would indicate in the case of an application for an interim injunction that the claimant's case is not urgent – see *Shepherd Homes Ltd v Sandham* [1971]. In *HP Bullmer Ltd v J Bollinger SA* [1977] which concerned the description of the defendants' goods as champagne perry, the court granted the claimants a perpetual injunction to restrain the use of the description (even though it had been used for over 40 years) because advice had had to be sought on the matter, and the wrong was a continuing one concerning a legal right. However, acquiescence by the claimant, who had knowledge of the violation of his rights, did bar the granting of an injunction in *Shaw v Applegate* [1977] because the defendant had been misled by the claimant's inactivity and damages were granted in lieu of the injunction.

Equity will not act in vain

An injunction will not be granted where it would be futile, eg see *Att. Gen. v Observer Ltd* [1990]. The Crown sought a perpetual injunction to prevent the publication of extracts of memoirs published in Australia by a former member of the British security service in breach of his duty of confidentiality. The injunction was refused because the memoirs *The Spycatcher* had already been published in Australia and the United States of America and were readily available.

The granting of an injunction must not cause undue hardship to the defendant

This is particularly relevant when the court considers whether to grant an interlocutory injunction where a full hearing of the case has not yet taken place. An injunction would not be granted if it caused hardship to an innocent third party.

Damages in lieu of an injunction

This jurisdiction is currently found in s 50 of the Senior Courts Act 1981.

However, the courts have been reluctant to award damages instead of an injunction because it allows a defendant to buy the right to continue with an unlawful act.

Guidance regarding when damages should be awarded in lieu of an injunction to restrain future unlawful conduct was provided by A.L. Smith LJ in *Shelfer v City of London Electric Lighting Co* [1985]. This was a case of nuisance brought by a pub lessee complaining of vibration and noise from the electric company's generators housed next door. A.L. Smith LJ set out what was described as a good working rule as to when damages should be awarded in lieu of an injunction, ie

(a) the injury to the claimant is small, and

(b) the injury is capable of being estimated in monetary terms; and

(c) the injury would be adequately compensated by a small payment;

(d) it would be oppressive to grant an injunction.

In subsequent cases, it has been emphasised that the guidance in *Shelfer* is adaptable to the facts of individual cases and does not constitute a rigid rule. However, the guidance in *Shelfer* remains good law and has been applied in many cases of trespass, nuisance and right to light since *Shelfer*, notably in *Jaggard v Sawyer* [1995] and more recently by the Court of Appeal in *Regan v Paul Properties Ltd* [2006].

> ▶ REGAN v PAUL PROPERTIES LTD [2006]
>
> **Basic facts**
>
> The appellant, Mr Regan, had complained that the respondent developers were infringing his right to light when they began developing two five storey properties directly across the road from his maisonette. He was told by the respondents, on the basis of incorrect professional advice, that the loss of light would be minor. The developers suspended completion of the fifth floor pending the outcome of the case. The Court of Appeal held that the loss of £5000 to the value of the appellant's property was not small, nor was it considered oppressive to require the respondents to remove part of the top floor at a cost of £35,000 which would reduce the value of that unit by £175,000.

Regarding the measure of damages, this should normally be compensatory for any future loss to the claimant because such loss would have been prevented had an injunction been granted. Thus in *Wrotham Park Estate v Parkside Homes* [1974], damages were based on the sum that the claimant could have expected for giving up her rights (ie for relaxing a restrictive covenant).

GENERAL PRINCIPLES REGARDING THE GRANTING OF INTERIM INJUNCTIONS

As an interim injunction is granted in the course of litigation before the court has heard all the evidence of the parties and fully considered the merits of the case, there must be clear principles governing such an order.

The principles were laid down by Lord Diplock in *American Cyanamid Co v Ethicon Ltd* [1975] as follows:

(a) The claimant must first adduce sufficient evidence to convince the court that his case is not frivolous or vexatious and that he has a good arguable case, ie there is a serious case to be tried with a real prospect of the claimant succeeding.

(b) Thereafter, the balance of convenience must be considered. This involves weighing up the risk of injustice to either party which may result from deciding the case before all the evidence has been heard at the full hearing.

   The court must consider the adequacy of damages to both parties, ie whether, if the claimant failed at the trial, any loss caused to the defendant by the grant of the interim injunction against him could be adequately compensated by damages. In this respect, the claimant, seeking the interim injunction is usually required to give an undertaking that he will compensate the defendant should he lose his case. Conversely, the court must also consider whether damages would adequately compensate the claimant for any loss caused by the defendant's acts if the interim injunction were not granted – *Express Newspaper Ltd v Keys* [1980].

(c) 'It is where there is doubt as to the adequacy of the respective remedies in damages available to either party or both, that the question of balance of convenience arises. It would be unwise to attempt even to list all the various factors which will need to be taken into consideration in deciding where the balance lies, let alone to suggest the relative weight to be attached to them. These will vary from case to case.' See *Hubbard v Pitt* [1976].

(d) 'Where other factors appear to be evenly balanced, it is a counsel of prudence to take such measures as are calculated to preserve the status quo.' The status quo is the state of affairs that existed immediately before the claim for an interim injunction.

Since the coming into force of the Human Rights Act 1998 on 2nd October 2000, the courts must have regard to the freedoms which the Act upholds, ie those contained in the European Convention on Human Rights. In particular when an injunction is sought to restrain publication, s 12(4) of the Act provides that the court must have particular regard to the importance of the Convention right to freedom of expression where the proceedings relate to journalistic, literary or artistic material, and the extent to which publication would be in the public interest. See *Douglas v Hello Ltd* [2001].

FREEZING ORDER

This is a specific type of prohibitory interim injunction and was formerly called a Mareva injunction after the case in which it was first applied – *Mareva Compania Naviera SA v International Bulk Carriers SA* [1980].

The essence of the freezing order is that the claimant should have a good arguable case against the defendant, whom he fears will move his assets out of the jurisdiction once proceedings are commenced against him. See *Polly Peck International v Nadir (No 2)* [1992]. For this reason, freezing orders are usually sought *ex parte* (without notice to the defendant) from a judge in chambers, which also ensures that the matter is dealt with swiftly. The claimant must make full disclosure of all material facts and give grounds for believing that the defendant has assets within the jurisdiction (eg a bank account, jewellery) which he believes will be removed from the jurisdiction, or destroyed or dissipated before the dispute is resolved. If the freezing order is granted, the defendant is prohibited from dealing with his assets in such a way so as to deprive the claimant of the possibility of enforcing the court's judgment against him.

In *Republic of Haiti v Duvalier* [1989] a worldwide freezing order was granted in respect of assets which were alleged to have been embezzled by the former President of Haiti.

SEARCH ORDER

A search order was formerly known as an Anton Piller order after the case in which it was introduced *Anton Piller KG v Manufacturing Processes Ltd* [1976]. The order, which was placed on a statutory basis by s 7 of the Civil Procedure Act 1997, allows the claimant to enter the defendant's premises and carry out a search for anything described in the order, eg documents, pirated tapes, pirated videos, and to make a copy or record of anything described in the order and to seize and retain for safe keeping anything described in the order.

As it is a draconian measure, it will be granted only if the claimant has an extremely strong *prima facie* case against the defendant, and there is clear evidence that the defendant has the relevant assets in his possession and there is a real risk that the defendant will destroy, conceal or dispose of those assets. See *Columbia Picture Industries Inc v Robinson* [1987].

The Practice Direction of July 1994 sets out certain requirements regarding the carrying out of the order, eg the order should be served by an experienced supervising solicitor, for example where the premises at which the order is to be served are likely to be occupied by a woman alone, the supervising solicitor, if a male, should be accompanied by a woman.

THE DECREE OF SPECIFIC PERFORMANCE

This is an order of the court which directs a party to a contract to perform his obligations under the contract, ie what he promised to do. As with the injunction, equity acts *in personam*, ie against the conscience of the wrongdoer.

As it is an equitable remedy, it is discretionary. The circumstances in which it will not be granted include the following.

1 Where damages would be an adequate remedy. Damages are not considered to be an adequate remedy in a contract for the sale of land as each piece of land is considered to be unique – compare chattels and stocks and shares. However, if the chattel is rare or of particular value to the claimant, specific performance may be granted – see *Sky-Petroleum v VIP Petroleum* [1974]. Section 52 of the Sale of Goods Act 1979 provides that in any action for breach of contract to deliver specific or ascertained goods, the court may, if it thinks fit, on the claimant's application, direct that the contract shall be performed specifically without giving the defendant the option of retaining the goods on payment of damages.

2 Where an order of specific performance would require constant supervision by the court. Therefore, the court will not normally order specific performance of building contracts – see *Co-operative Insurance Society Ltd v Argyll Stores (Holdings) Ltd* [1998].

3 For contracts of personal service, s 236 of the Trade Union and Labour Relations (Consolidation) Act 1992 provides that no court shall by way of an order for specific performance compel an employee to do any work or to attend at any place for the doing of any work. For contracts which are not governed by the Act, the order will not be granted because it is contrary to

public policy to force a person to work for another – it is tantamount to slavery, and also such an order would require constant supervision.

4   Where there is a lack of mutuality. Thus specific performance will not usually be granted unless the remedy is mutual. A minor cannot obtain an order for specific performance because it cannot be decreed against him.

5   Where the claimant acted inequitably. The maxim 'He who comes to equity must come with clean hands' applies. The claimant must prove that he has performed his obligations under the contract, or is ready and willing to perform them.

6   Where the order would cause undue hardship to the defendant or a third party. See *Patel v Ali* [1984].

7   Where the claimant has unduly delayed. The six year limitation period for an action based on a simple contract does not apply. Instead, the claimant must have regard to the doctrine of laches, ie delay by the claimant in bringing proceedings may defeat his claim for specific performance – *Patel v Ali* [1984].

You should now be confident that you would be able to tick all of the boxes on the checklist at the beginning of this chapter. To check your knowledge of Equitable remedies of injunction and specific performance why not visit the companion website and take the Multiple Choice Question test. Check your understanding of the terms and vocabulary used in this chapter with the flashcard glossary.

13

Putting it into practice ...

Now that you've mastered the basics, you will want to put it all into practice. The Routledge Questions and Answers series provides an ideal opportunity for you to apply your understanding and knowledge of the law and to hone your essay-writing technique.

We've included one exam-style essay question, which replicates the type of question posed in the Routledge Questions and Answers series to give you some essential exam practice. The Q&A includes an answer plan and a fully worked model answer to help you recognise what examiners might look for in your answer.

QUESTION 1

'Although equity will not aid a volunteer, it will not strive officiously to defeat a gift' (*per* Lord Browne-Wilkinson in *Choithram International SA v Pagarani* [2001]).

▧ **Evaluate this statement by reference to decided cases.**

AIM HIGHER
Students are urged to read the judgments in the controversial decision *Pennington v Waine*. In this case, Arden LJ's view of unconscionability was based on the discretion of the court and varies with the circumstances of each case. This approach introduces notions of justice and fairness in outcomes to transactions that involve the process of the transfer of the legal title to property. In *Pennington v Waine*, what would have been the position if registration of the shares was declined by the company? If the constructive trust theory is to be maintained, despite the refusal to register the new owner, this would result in equity treating an ineffective transfer as a valid declaration of trust. But in *Pennington v Waine* the donor had not declared a trust, nor made a gift, nor had she done everything in her power to make a gift, yet the court decided that the transfer was effective in equity.

Common Pitfalls
Students are urged to approach this question by highlighting the various occasions when the court in purporting to apply the *Milroy v Lord* principle, in effect, extended the test in a number of landmark decisions.

Simply 'trotting out' the popular cases without a structure will not stand you in good stead with the examiners. Students should be clear as to the significance of the principles in the controversial decisions, *Choithram v Pagarani*, *Pennington v Waine* and *Fletcher v Fletcher*.

Answer Plan

- The *Milroy v Lord* test.

- Transferor completing everything required of him.

- No self-declaration following imperfect transfer.

- The principle in *Re Ralli*.

- Multiple trustees, including the settlor.

- Trust of a chose in action.

- Consequences of a trust being perfect.

- Exceptions to the rule that equity will not assist a volunteer.

ANSWER

This statement by Lord Browne-Wilkinson highlights two fundamental principles of equity: the notion that equity will not assist a volunteer and that there is no policy in equity to defeat a perfect gift. These are self-evident propositions. However, a number of landmark cases have striven to perfect gifts which, on orthodox theory, ought to be considered as imperfect.

The principle laid down by Turner LJ in *Milroy v Lord* [1862] identifies the various modes of creating an express trust. Generally, there are two modes of constituting an express trust and the onus is on the settlor to execute one (or in exceptional circumstances both) of these modes for carrying out his intention. The two modes of creating an express trust are:

(a) a self-declaration of trust; and

(b) a transfer of property to the trustees, subject to a direction to hold upon trust for the beneficiaries.

A settlor may declare that he presently holds specific property on trust, indicating the interest, for a beneficiary. In this respect he simply retains the property as trustee for the relevant beneficiaries. Clear evidence is needed to convert the status of the original owner of the property to that of a trustee. This form of creating an express trust is as effective as the transfer and declaration mode. In the absence of specific statutory provisions to the contrary, no special form is required as long as the intention of the settlor is sufficiently clear to constitute himself a trustee, for 'equity looks at the intent rather than the form'. Thus, the declaration of trust may be in writing or may be evidenced by conduct or may take the form of a verbal statement or a combination of each of these types of evidence: see *Paul v Constance* [1977]; contrast *Jones v Lock* [1865]. What is required from the settlor is a firm commitment on his part to undertake the duties of trusteeship in respect of the relevant property for the benefit of the specified beneficiaries. The effect of this mode of creation is to alter the status of the settlor from a beneficial owner to that of a trustee. The test that is applicable here is the 'three certainties' test, ie certainty of intention, subject matter and objects.

The alternative mode of creating an express trust involves a transfer of the relevant property to another person (or persons) as trustee(s), subject to a valid declaration of trust. In this context the settlor must comply with two require-ments, namely a transfer of the relevant property or interest to the trustees complemented with a declaration of the terms of the trust. If the settlor intends to create a trust by this method and declares the terms of the trust, but fails to transfer the property to the intended trustees, it is clear that no express trust is created. The court will not automatically imply a self-declaration of trust, see *Richards v Delbridge* [1874] and *Jones v Lock* [1865].

The formal requirements, if any, concerning the transfer of the legal title or equitable title to property vary with the nature of the property involved, in accordance with the *Milroy v Lord* [1862] principle; but if the transferor has done everything required of him to transfer the legal title to property and something has yet to be done by a third party, the transfer will be effective in equity, see *Re Rose* [1952], contrast *Re Fry* [1946] in respect of the transfer of shares in a private company. The effect of this rule (known as the rule in *Re Rose*) is that although the transfer of the legal title is not complete, the trans-feror will nevertheless hold the legal title to the property as constructive trustee for the transferee. It is unclear as to the precise role played by the third party. Some third parties may have a purely ministerial role while others may have a discretion to refuse registration of the legal title. It would appear that the *Re*

Rose principle is applicable irrespective of the role of the third party – dispositive or not. In *Mascall v Mascall* [1984], the rule was extended to a delivery by the transferor of a registered land certificate and duly executed transfer form to the transferee. Indeed, in *Pennington v Waine* [2002], the Court of Appeal decided that the delivery of the share transfer form to the company could be dispensed with. If it would be *unconscionable* for the transferor to have recalled what she intended to donate, the transfer would be effective in equity. This notion of unconscionability was based on analogy with the principle laid down by the Privy Council in *Choithram International SA v Pagarani* [2001]. However, the Privy Council in that case had decided that the trust was perfectly created and thus it would have been unconscionable for the settlor to deny the existence of the trust, whereas in *Pennington* the donor had neither declared a trust nor made a perfect gift nor had she done everything required of her to make the gift. Accordingly, *Pennington* was an unjustifiable extension of the *Milroy v Lord* principle.

In *Re Ralli* [1964], the High Court decided that a settlor may expressly manifest an intention to transfer the relevant property to third-party trustees (transfer and declaration mode) and, prior to completing the transfer, to declare himself a trustee for the beneficiaries (self-declaration mode). In this event, the trust will be perfect, provided that the third-party trustee acquires the property during the settlor's lifetime. In other words, the self-declaration of trust is regarded as conditional on an effective transfer of the property to the third-party trustee. This condition is required to be satisfied during the lifetime of the settlor in order to perfect the trust, ie to render it unconscionable for the settlor to reclaim the property. The court had also decided that it was immaterial how the third-party trustee acquired the relevant property. The mere fact that the property had reached the hands of the intended trustees was sufficient to constitute the trust. The logic of this test extended the *Milroy v Lord* principle. In addition, the court decided on a separate ground that the rule in *Strong v Bird* [1874] (imperfect *inter vivos* gifts where the will appoints the donee as executor) was extended to residuary gifts created in a will.

Moreover, in *Choithram International SA v Pagarani* [2001], the Privy Council decided that where the settlor appoints multiple trustees, including himself, and declares a present, unconditional and irrevocable intention to create a trust for specific persons, a failure to transfer the property to the nominated trustees is not fatal, for his (settlor's) retention of the property will be treated as a trustee.

Trusteeship for these purposes is treated as a joint office so that the acquisition of the property by one trustee is equivalent to its acquisition by all the trustees. There was no distinction between a settlor declaring himself to be the sole trustee and one of a number of trustees.

In *Fletcher v Fletcher* [1844], the court construed the subject matter of a covenant (to transfer property on trust) as creating a chose in action, namely the benefit of the covenant. This intangible property right may be transferred to the trustees on trust for the relevant beneficiaries thus perfecting the trust. What is needed to assign such a right or chose is a clear intention on the part of the assignor to dispose of the chose to the transferee, but it is questionable whether the settlor had the benefit of the covenant. However, the *Fletcher* principle was subsequently restricted in *Re Cook* [1965] to debts enforceable at law, as distinct from any other choses in action.

Where a trust is perfectly created, the beneficiary is given a right *in rem* in the trust property and may protect his interest against anyone, except a *bona fide* transferee of the legal estate for value without notice. In short he has a *locus standi* to enforce the trust, simply by proving that he is an authorised equitable owner of the property. He may bring the claim in his own name and is entitled to join the trustee as a co-defendant. On the other hand, if the intended trust is imperfect, the transaction operates as an agreement to create a trust. This involves the law of contract, as opposed to the law of trust. An agreement to create a trust may only be enforced in equity by non-volunteers. The rule is that 'equity will not assist a volunteer' and 'equity will not perfect an imperfect gift'. To obtain an equitable remedy, the claimant is required to establish that he has furnished consideration. Valuable consideration refers either to common law consideration in money or money's worth or marriage consideration in equity. Common law consideration is the price paid by each party to an agreement. 'Marriage consideration' takes the form of an ante-nuptial settlement made in consideration of marriage, or a post-nuptial settlement made in pursuance of an ante-nuptial agreement. The persons who are treated as providing marriage consideration are the parties to the marriage and the issue of the marriage, including remoter issue.

It follows that if the trust is imperfect and the claimant wishes to obtain equitable assistance, he is required to demonstrate that he has furnished valuable consideration. If this is the case, the imperfect trust will be treated to all intents and purposes as though it was perfect. In other words, the claimant who has furnished valuable consideration will derive from the agreement to create a trust all the benefits accorded to a beneficiary under a perfect trust, see *Pullan v Koe* [1913].

On the other hand, where the claimant is a volunteer and a non-covenantee, the court refused to issue directions in his favour to enforce the covenant at law on the ground that the volunteer ought not to obtain relief indirectly when he could not obtain the same directly, see *Re Pryce* [1917]. In *Re Kay* [1939], the court extended the principle further by preventing the volunteer non-covenantee from bringing a claim in damages. The Contracts (Rights of Third Parties) Act 1999 has modified this principle only to the extent that it allows a non-party to a contract to bring a claim in his own right. If he is a volunteer the remedy will be damages.

However, there are well-established exceptions to the general rule that equity will not assist a volunteer such as the rule in *Strong v Bird* [1874], *donatio mortis causa* (DMC) and proprietary estoppel.